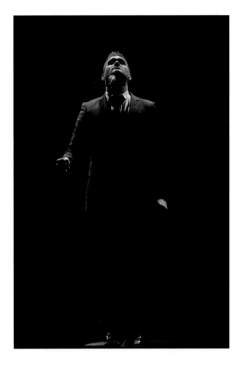

# michael bublé
## *crazy life*

OLIVIA KING

# michael bublé

*crazy life*

# contents

# introduction

I t's a Saturday night and Michael Bublé has just given the performance of his life in front of thousands of fans. He is charismatic and debonair – the very essence of suave sophistication, just as you'd imagine from the smooth, jazzy, dreamy blues that he sings.

Between the songs, Michael skips across the stage and banters with the audience. He leans down and shakes the hand of a young girl in the front row, and poses for photographs with some screaming fans. This is no ordinary concert.

The applause is deafening. And at that moment, it is hard to imagine him anywhere else but on the stage, singing and performing. The endless romantic, who wears his heart on his sleeve, and refuses to censor himself for the media. His loose lips and quick wit have got him into trouble with the press countless times, but he never learns his lesson.

So how did this hockey-mad kid from Burnaby in British Columbia first come to hold a microphone, or set foot on a stage? Michael's story is a true tale of an ambitious kid making a bright future happen for himself.

Michael's love of all things jazz and blues started early, care of his grandpa Mitch, who filled the Bublé house with popular tunes from his youth: the songs that would come to define Michael's sound, by singers like Frank Sinatra, Bobby Darin and Paul Anka. Bitten by the music bug from a young age,

Michael's love developed from merely appreciating the music to wanting to interpret the songs himself – at first, singing into his sister's hairbrush, but eventually seeking the bright lights of the stage.

Michael has sung in front of thousands of people, in every situation you can imagine. From dimly lit jazz clubs in downtown Vancouver to the sterile stage of a cruise liner, Michael spent his late teens and early twenties with his nose to the grindstone. He played every gig he was offered, and sang at every available opportunity, patiently waiting for his big break. But try as he might – and wait as he might – for a long time that big break eluded him.

In desperation, Michael decided to abandon his musical dreams to pursue a career in journalism. He took one last gig to earn the money to pay for his flight back home – and it was at this very show that he got his break. An aide for the former Canadian prime minister Brian Mulroney was in the crowd and asked Michael for a CD, later passing it on to the former prime minister, who loved it. Mulroney got in touch and asked Michael to sing at his daughter's wedding, where he was introduced to Grammy Award-winning record producer, David Foster.

And the rest is history – multi-platinum-album-selling, award-winning, history. From his early years and all those false starts, to the red carpets, swanky showbiz parties and an ultimate celebrity lifestyle, find out all the ups and downs in Michael's journey as the son of a fisherman became the international singing sensation that he is today.

# a happy childhood

Michael Bublé was born on 9 September 1975, on the north-west coast of Canada. The oldest of three children, Michael and his younger sisters Brandee and Crystal spent their childhood days chasing each other around the house. The Bublé household was a close-knit family unit who all loved each other dearly. Music was an important part of life for the Bublé clan, mostly due to the influence of grandpa Mitch, an Italian immigrant, who played melodies from the 1940s and 1950s in the background of family life.

Grandpa Mitch raised his grandchildren on the classics, playing Frank Sinatra in the house from morning until night. Because dad Lewis was a fisherman and spent his summers away at sea, Michael and his sisters would often go over to their grandparents' house, where Mitch would play them all the songs he loved. Michael and his sisters liked to sing, and learned all the words to the songs they heard there. The swinging sounds of Rosemary Clooney and Bobby Darin echoed around the house as Mitch bounced young Michael on his knee, and rocked him to sleep.

At Christmas, family tradition dictated that the Bublés always listened to Bing Crosby's 'White Christmas'. Young Michael was entranced by the magical sound of the song, and it wasn't long before he was listening to it – and other

Bing Crosby classics – all year round. This was Michael's first introduction to the world of classic croon and he was instantly hooked.

'Even at that young age I thought the words were something I could understand and the melodies were so catchy,' Michael later said in an interview with *Smooth Jazz Now*. 'For me, that feeling of a group … when they're swinging and stuff, it's something that you feel through your whole body, and you can't stop tapping your knee. That's pretty much what I live for and I always did and I've always felt that way.'

Although Michael loved the old classics, he also idolised more contemporary artists like Michael Jackson. He learned all the words to 'Man In The Mirror' and performed using his sister Brandee's hairbrush as a microphone, much to the amusement of both his sisters! At nights, he dreamed of being a singer when he grew up, singing to thousands of people in huge auditoriums across the world. Was it a premonition, or did this young boy from rural Canada actually manage to make his dreams come true?

As a child, Michael attended Seaforth Elementary School and Cariboo Hill Secondary School. He was a sporty kid who enjoyed the rough and tumble of the hockey pitch. He loved watching the Vancouver Canucks with his dad Lewis, and attended their home games religiously. He had ambitions of being an ice-hockey player when he grew up, but as a player of average ability, he wasn't good enough to have made a career from it.

Hockey aspirations aside, sport remained a big love for the young boy. When he was eight years old, dad Lewis took him on a special trip to watch the Harlem Globetrotters basketball team. When the game was over, one of the players came over to young Michael, who was sat in the audience, and brandished a bucket. Michael was super scared, thinking they were about to dump a bucket of water over his head, but as the player overturned the bucket, thousands of tiny pieces of confetti fluttered out. Being chosen from the crowd like that was one of the biggest moments of his life, and it stuck with the young boy as he grew into a man.

But however much Michael liked sport, music was always his first love. In his early teens he listened to a lot of rock and hip hop, like the Beastie Boys and Guns N' Roses. But around the age of 14 he started remembering the music he'd heard as a child and began digging around in his grandpa's old record collection. Michael was hungry for lyrics and melodies that really meant something to him.

'My grandfather was really my best friend growing up,' Michael later told the *Daily Post*. 'He was the one who opened me up to a whole world of music that seemed to have been passed over by my generation. Although I like rock and roll and modern music, the first time my granddad played me the Mills Brothers something magical happened. The lyrics were so romantic, so real, the way a song should be for me. It was like seeing my future flash before me. I wanted to be a singer and I knew that this was the music that I wanted to sing.'

At the impressionable age of 14, Michael spent the summer working alongside his dad as a crewman on salmon-fishing boats. It was hard, physical work, but it taught Michael about responsibility and what it meant to be a man. Working on the boat during the summer meant that Michael was sometimes away from home for two or three months at a time. But he was

never far from music. Before he set off on his first long voyage, grandpa Mitch hugged him goodbye and pressed a small package into his hands.

'Sunshine,' he said, using his nickname for Michael, 'take these tapes and listen to them. It's the music I loved when I was young – and I know you'll love it too.'

The package contained tapes full of classic jazz and blues by artists like Ella Fitzgerald, the Mills Brothers and Louis Armstrong. Michael listened on repeat to the song 'I Left My Heart In San Francisco' by Tony Bennett, and Bennett soon became one of his favourite artists. Michael could never have imagined, sitting on that fishing boat, that just a few years in the future he would actually get to meet and sing with his idol!

In between the fishing shifts, there were endless hours of doing nothing, but Michael filled all his time with the music he had been given. Sometimes he would trade tapes with other workers on the boat; students from Canadian universities, jazz-mad kids working abroad during their summer holiday.

As well as listening to music on the boat, Michael was also performing – even though his audience, very often, consisted of nothing but the sparkling waves of the ocean and the clear blue sky. 'Every single day I sang. Really, I didn't shut up,' he said later. 'I remember sitting on the bow of the boat, by the coiled ropes by the anchor, singing away and just dreaming of fame.'

He found being on the boat hard work. 'I know what it's like to have a tough job so it makes me really appreciate the fact that all I have to do now is get up on stage and sing with great musicians.'

'Hard work' was an understatement: working on the boat was physically demanding, exhausting manual labour. 'Man, it was hard,' Michael said in an interview with *Saturday Night*. 'We'd be outside, 4 a.m., pouring rain. I'd be sitting there freezing cold, tired, sick, just dying. I'd cry and say to my dad, "How could you make your son come out here?" I was terrified I'd have to work like he did.' It was all the more reason for Michael to withdraw into his dreams of being a famous singer – he didn't want to spend his years working in the way his father had.

That Christmas was when Michael's mum Amber realised her son had a special gift. All the kids were musical, but driving to the store with the three of them harmonising Christmas carols in the back of the car, she was

'I remember sitting on the bow of the boat, by the coiled ropes by the anchor, singing away and just dreaming of fame'

suddenly struck by how much Michael's voice stood out. All three of her children sounded great, but she realised that Michael had real talent.

As a teen, Michael was hip to everything that was in the charts – all the music his friends were listening to. He had long hair, two earrings through each ear, stonewashed jeans and high-top trainers. He wore a denim jacket that he had scribbled all over with marker pen, writing slogans like 'I Love Guns N' Roses' and 'I Love AC/DC'.

But when listening to songs like Vic Damone's version of 'It Had To Be You', Michael knew there was something about those songs that really spoke to him. He heard the melody wrapped around lyrics that were a perfect fit, in Vic's beautiful singing voice, and it didn't matter how old the song was or that none of his friends were into it. Listening to old classics was a way for young Michael to follow his own beat and not be one of the sheep blindly following the herd and listening only to what was supposedly cool.

After a couple of years of working summers on the boat, immersing himself in music, Michael was adamant that he wanted to be a professional singer. He slept with a Bible under his pillow and prayed at night for his dream to come true. When Mitch bought him a karaoke set, Michael proved that he could not only sing but perform like a star, too. 'He used to sing with a broom handle as a microphone. He was a born performer, a real hambone!' Mitch later told *Saturday Night*. 'Then, one Boxing Day ... he started singing "New York, New York" with his karaoke set. He floored me. I thought, this guy's really got talent.'

With a little emotional blackmail, Mitch encouraged his grandson to sing some of the jazz greats. 'Oh sunshine,' he said to the teenager. 'Can you just learn the Bobby Darin greatest hits, and learn the song "Clementine"? I'm an old man and I'd love to hear them before I die...'

Mitch was a plumber, and started swapping plumbing jobs to try and help his grandson develop his talent. He paid for Michael to have singing lessons with opera baritone Joseph Shore, and he also helped young Michael get his first gigs. Aged 16, Michael was too young to be allowed into nightclubs to perform, but some persuasive words from Mitch, and the offer of fixing their toilets for free, meant that Michael was soon performing cover versions of his favourite jazz records in clubs around his home city of Burnaby.

Burnaby isn't a huge place – it has a population of just under 200,000 – but Michael always kept his eye on the nearby city of Vancouver. A huge, sprawling metropolis that is home to well over a million people, Michael knew that Vancouver had more venues, clubs and theatres than Burnaby. He kept his eye on leaflets and posters advertising any potential opportunities – in the big city or in his hometown. He didn't have to wait long. One day, walking home from school, Michael saw a poster advertising a talent contest. Elated, he ripped the poster off the wall and ran home to tell his parents that he was going to enter.

Michael's parents and Mitch went along with him to the show. Michael was super nervous, but as he mounted the stage, he looked down and saw his grandpa, who winked at him, and he knew it would be okay.

As soon as Michael walked up the rickety wooden steps onto the stage, he felt his heart beating in his throat and his mouth go dry. But he cleared his throat, and as soon as he started singing, he felt a sudden rush of endorphins. It was unlike anything he'd ever felt before. Although he didn't win the contest, Michael was completely hooked on the feeling of being on stage, and started singing at every given opportunity.

This even included singing while he was at work. In his mid-teens, as well as working on the boat, he occasionally worked behind the till at a climbing gym that his dad Lewis part-owned. Alongside his task of ringing through sales, Michael was often found singing to girls who had come in, serenading them with Sinatra as they blushed and giggled and begged for him to sing them another song, a request that he could never refuse.

In fact, girls were a big part of why young Michael wanted to get into the music business in the first place. 'I would love to tell you that I was this wonderfully smart and full-of-integrity kinda guy,' he admitted in an interview with the *Telegraph*. 'But at the same time, man, I wanted to get laid. That was a big part of it! This is why I wanted to be different and why I wanted to have power and fame and money: because I wanted to be attractive to the opposite sex. I'd be lying to you if I didn't say that was a big part of it.'

As well as helping to satisfy Michael's desire for the opposite sex, his angelic voice also got him out of some sticky situations. One summer, when on a fishing job with his father, Michael and the other crew members took a bus into a small town to relax onshore and have a drink. Michael led them to a local karaoke night. The crowd were a tough-looking bunch and the rest of the crew were in fear of their lives. It even looked for a second like it might turn nasty. But fearless Michael was determined to sing, so he got on stage and did his best on a number of Elvis songs. He was a big hit, and by the end of the night, the crowd all bought him drinks!

According to an interview in *Smooth Jazz Now*, Michael entered another competition when he was 18, even though the rules said all entrants had to be 19. He won the competition, but the organiser disqualified him for being underage. The organiser's name was Beverly Delich, a local businesswoman and entrepreneur. She was so impressed by Michael's performance that she later called him at home and told him she thought he should enter the Canadian Youth Talent Search.

The Canadian Youth Talent Search was an annual event that had started in 1981, to celebrate the performing-arts talents of Canada's youth. Young Canadians between the ages of 13 and 21 battled it out through different stages of the contest – from local to the provincial areas, then on to the National Finals. Having just missed the contest for that year, it wasn't until he turned 20 that Michael was able to compete for his local area. He progressed easily through the local and provincial heats, and when he arrived at the finals, he was more excited than nervous, realising that he had a real shot of winning.

All the contestants were judged on their natural ability, the quality of their performance, their stage presence, and audience rapport. Michael had always been a charmer – almost like he was born with a silver tongue – and had a strong connection with the audience immediately. The judges loved him, and he was the clear winner of the show. As Michael walked up the ornate mahogany steps onto the stage to accept his prize and bow to the audience,

he thought to himself how he would never have entered the Canadian Youth Talent Search at all if it hadn't been for Bev.

She was the first person he'd come across who had the knowledge and the contacts to help him progress his career. There was only one way he could see himself moving forward, and that was if she would be his manager. So, on the plane back from the contest, Michael asked her if she'd consider taking him on as a client, and helping him shape his musical career.

Bev was amused. Here was a young man with nothing behind him except a great voice and a burning desire. But Michael's charm and persuasiveness were already well developed. Bev asked him why he thought he needed a manager. With his characteristic cheekiness, Michael told her that he was going to be a great success, and he would give her 15 per cent of everything he ever earned. Bev suppressed a smile, and said to Michael: 'What's 15 per cent of nothing?'

But Michael persisted and eventually Bev gave in, and helped him record three independent demo albums that he could sell at his shows or give away to raise his profile. Michael paid for the recording and production of the CDs himself with cash he'd earned from his different jobs.

He was so determined that he would perform anywhere that he was allowed to play – conventions, cruise ships, musical theatre performances, in shopping malls. He even performed as a singing telegram, turning up at restaurants to sing love songs or 'Happy Birthday' to someone. But because he was usually hired to embarrass the person he was singing to, his subtle and quiet voice didn't really do the job and many of his clients refused to pay him. Eventually he decided he wasn't suited to that line of work and quit the singing telegram business altogether.

In 1997, Michael did manage to find regular paid work at the BaBalu Lounge, a nightclub in downtown Vancouver. Every Sunday and Monday night for two years, he performed with the Smokin' Section band. It was this regular gig at BaBalu that gave Michael the experience he needed to fine-tune his craft.

The audience might have been there to hook up or get drunk, but it gave Michael the space to experiment and learn what worked on stage. 'It taught me how not to reek of desperation, how to step back and try to be charismatic and let them fall in love with me,' he later said of his time at BaBalu. The nightclub was so important to him that he named his second independent album after it (the previous one was titled *First Dance* and the third was called *Dream*). Though the Vancouver nightspot burned to the ground in 2001, this humble place was a building-block for the singer who would later dominate the charts across the world.

After months of grafting, with his low-profile gigs and some small TV parts, Michael finally got a bigger break, landing a role in a musical that was touring Vancouver.

It was in rehearsals for the musical that Michael got friendly with a pretty brunette called Debbie Timuss who was in the show. Michael hadn't had much experience in dancing, so Debbie took him under her wing and showed him all the moves.

After a couple of years, Debbie and Michael eventually started dating, and moved to Toronto to perform in *Forever Swing*, a musical that was touring across Canada. The show received good reviews, with particular attention paid to Michael, whose voice stood out amongst the rest of the cast.

## After months of grafting, Michael finally got a bigger break.

There were lots of opportunities for Debbie in Toronto. She was an actress, a singer and a dancer, perfectly suited to work in the big city. Michael thought that moving to a bigger city would mean there was more chance of something happening for him, but at age 25, he was having trouble finding his niche – and trouble paying the rent. All the shows he played at – corporate events or late-night lounges – weren't filled with music lovers; they were just full of people who wanted to get drunk and weren't bothered about the music at all. The couple relied on Debbie's work to pay their bills, and Michael was so frustrated that he seriously considered quitting music and pursuing journalism instead.

Bev told the *Globe and Mail* that Michael had called her in the middle of the night, in desperate need of some advice.

'Michael, go ahead,' Bev had told him. 'In a few years, when you see some other singer creeping up, making it big with the same songs you sing, you'll regret it for the rest of your life.'

Bev tried to persuade Michael to give his career another year. Michael wasn't sure: he felt like he had been banging his head against a brick wall for years and years, and that it was never going to happen for him.

Michael had run out of money, and run out of options. He decided to fly back to Vancouver, move back in with his family and put himself through journalism school. The only problem was that he didn't even have enough money for the flight home.

So, he had to work. He was offered a job singing at a business dinner, which offered a handsome fee of $1,000, enough to fly him and girlfriend Debbie back to Vancouver. The gig was pretty average, but Michael always put everything into every performance, treating it like he was on stage in Vegas, no matter where he was. Afterwards, a man who had been in the audience came up to him and shook his hand, telling him how much he'd enjoyed the show.

Michael thanked him, and reached into his bag, where he had the last copy of his self-produced CD. 'If you like it, take it home and listen to it with your wife and kids,' he said, signing it. Then, with his trademark sense of humour, Michael added: 'If you don't like it, it'll make a great coaster for your desk!'

The next day, Michael was lying in bed, feeling fairly depressed about the general state of his life, when the phone rang. It was Michael McSweeney, the man he'd met at the show the night before, who had taken a copy of his CD. It turned out that McSweeney was a speech-writer and aide to the former Canadian prime minister, Brian Mulroney. McSweeney had listened to the CD and loved it, and felt that Brian would love it too, so he had passed it on. Brian Mulroney did love the CD, and wanted to ask Michael to play at his daughter's wedding reception. At first Michael refused – he thought that singing at weddings would jinx him – but eventually he was persuaded after he found out that there would be some influential people from the music industry attending.

It was to be a night that would change his life.

Brian Mulroney loved Michael's voice and the songs that he sang – they reminded him of the golden days of his own youth. He was determined to get Michael as much exposure at his daughter's wedding as he could. The guest list was packed with influential figures from the world of pop music – people who could help Michael get his lucky break. Among those on the guest list for the ceremony was David Foster, a famous and talented record producer, the man behind best-selling records by Whitney Houston, Madonna, Celine Dion and Barbra Streisand.

Michael watched nervously from the side of the stage, just before he went on, as Brian Mulroney walked over to David Foster and stood by his side. 'When David Foster came in I could see his face as I started singing and I knew he was thinking, "Oh Lord! Here we go!"' Michael laughed in an interview with *Smooth Jazz Now*. 'Brian Mulroney had his arm around David and was shaking him, saying "Watch him, isn't he great? Just watch him." So, he really kind of forced me upon David.'

David wasn't sure at first – thinking that Michael would be just another average wedding singer. But when he heard Michael sing, he was transfixed.

The day after the wedding, Brian – who had quickly become Michael's number-one fan – hosted a brunch for the guests that had travelled from out of town, and invited Michael to sing again. David Foster had enough experience behind him to know that Michael was a hugely talented singer, but he was unsure about his potential as a pop star. After all, how would they mass-market a lounge singer to the pop-hungry public? Nevertheless, he invited Michael to his studio in Malibu to hang out and record some material.

After a couple of days of working together, David still didn't quite know how they would make a star of Michael. He scratched his head behind the mixing desk, then crossed his arms and sighed. 'Michael,' he said, 'you're a lovely entertainer and have a nice voice, but there's nothing I can do for you.'

But Michael and his manager Bev had seen a glimmer of hope for his career, and they weren't about to let this opportunity go so easily. Both Michael and Bev moved to Los Angeles for an entire year, practically stalking David Foster to prove how serious they were. 'I drove him nuts!' Michael admitted in an interview with *Macleans*. 'I'd constantly drive out to his home and ask, "When are you gonna sign me?"'

Though David Foster was adamant at first that they couldn't work together, he did want to support the young singer, and managed to direct some corporate industry gigs in Michael's direction. While Michael was in LA, he also won the role of Van (a singer and nightclub owner) in the movie comedy *Totally Blonde*. Although not a massive box-office hit, it was good exposure for Michael, who sang several songs throughout the film.

Michael and Bev refused point blank to leave Los Angeles until David had agreed to work with Michael. While they were down there, Michael had constant contact from his newest greatest fans, the Mulroneys. 'Mila and Brian

would phone and say, "I just put a call in to David so we're putting the heat on him." They were so supportive,' Michael later remembered. 'He went way out of his way to help me.'

Michael was not the only young Canadian singer that Mila and Brian had introduced to David Foster. Some years prior, they had also introduced a young French Canadian singer to him, named Celine Dion.

Eventually, the combined persistence of Michael and Bev, and calls from Brian and Mila Mulroney, paid off, and David started looking for a way to help Michael. David's many connections in the music industry meant he could call on the help of a seasoned professional in shaping Michael's career. Paul Anka, a fellow Canadian, had been a famous teen pop singer in the 1950s, and had written a slew of classics that Michael counted amongst his favourite songs. David arranged for the two of them to meet, and they hit it off straight away. David asked Paul if he would take Michael on as a student – to guide him along the tough road to stardom that lay ahead of him.

'I went to his hotel and met him and it was just great,' said Michael. 'He is a super nice guy and I have enjoyed having him as a friend. It is an amazing thing to be able to pick up the phone and say, "Hey Paul, how are you, I am a little nervous about this gig and what do you think I should open with and do you think I should talk here or there?" How cool is it that I get to call Paul Anka, who has done this for so long and is so great at it, and I get to ask him advice on what I should do. God has been good to me.'

Before anything else could happen, half a million dollars had to be raised to pay for the demo. In the summer of 2001, Bev started looking for a private investor to back the project. An article in *Macleans* stated that Paul Anka had a mysterious benefactor lined up to fund it, but then David Foster had a last-minute change of heart, and decided to pay for the demos himself, leaving it up to the Warner Bros. executives to choose whether or not to sign Michael.

With funding secured, there was just one small thing left to do: get into the studio and start recording.

# michael bublé – a brilliant debut

**A**s 2002 drew to a close, Michael spent weeks in the studio with producer David Foster. They went through hundreds of old records that had formed the basis of Michael's childhood introduction to music – songs he had grown up with, songs he was in love with.

David had decided to find well-known and well-loved classics and rework them with a modern twist – a 'Bublé' twist. His aim was to find a happy medium, pleasing the audiences who already knew the songs, while introducing a whole new generation to them.

David knew that if they could record a good demo album, they would have their best shot at convincing Warner Bros. that Michael was worth their time. Michael's winning way with words also came into play to convince the label to sign him – he vowed to 'work his ass off' to fill the slot left open by modern crooner Harry Connick Jr, who left singing to concentrate on his film career.

'Michael hasn't just learned this music,' David was quoted as saying in the *Manila Bulletin*, 'He's lived it. He brings youthful energy to it, tough and tender at the same time and like nothing else I've ever heard. The great thing is, he's tapped into a repertoire that can last him fifty years. He's at the beginning of a very long career.'

As they settled into work in the studio, Michael, David, producer-partner Humberto Gatica and Paul Anka all put their heads together to come up with a list of tracks that would display the full range of Michael's vocal talents.

Michael was 'more of a purest' than the others when it came to exploring potential songs, and wasn't initially comfortable with the idea of covering 'How Do You Mend A Broken Heart' by the Bee Gees, or the Lou Rawls' song 'You'll Never Find'.

'I thought, "I don't want to do these songs. I don't want to be known as a strange lounge act going over the line of good taste,"' Michael later said in an interview with *Smooth Jazz Now*. 'It's funny – David looked at me and said, "No man, these are good tunes, good melodies and good words make for a timeless tune. Anything can work and if it's a timeless tune it will lend itself to the style of the genre that you love." So everyone got what they wanted out of it. I got my standards out of it and they got their newer stuff.'

An experienced producer, David Foster had a meticulous and careful way of working. He recorded multiple takes of each track that Michael sang. Afterwards he would carefully cut what he thought was the most perfectly sung phrase from each different take and then paste them all together into one vocal track – rather like putting together an enormous audio jigsaw puzzle. The end result was a finished song where Michael's vocals had actually been recorded at completely different times.

Track One was 'Fever', a rhythm and blues classic originally recorded by Little Willie John in 1956. The song had since been covered by countless recording artists, most notably Madonna and Elvis Presley. Michael gave the song a smoky vibe, kicking the album off in x-rated fashion.

Track Two was Van Morrison's 'Moondance', originally recorded in 1969, not released as a single until 1977, and named in *Rolling Stone*'s 500 Greatest Songs of All Time. Michael's version introduced the big-band sound he loved so much, and was a live favourite.

Introducing a more contemporary artist to the mix, Track Three was George Michael's 'Kissing A Fool'. A far cry from George's power pop, the ballad had always been one of Michael's favourite songs, and he was thrilled at the opportunity to cover it.

Track Four on the album was 'For Once In My Life', a song written by Ron Miller and Orlando Murden for Motown Records in 1967. The song – originally a slow-tempo ballad – has been covered by a number of different artists, though the most famous version was recorded by Stevie Wonder in 1968. Michael took the song back to its original roots, recording a slow-tempo version that brought a tear to the eyes of the crowd when it was performed live.

Track Five on the album was the Bee Gees' hit single 'How Can You Mend A Broken Heart'. The song was a tribute to the original Bee Gees' hit (and to the Bee Gees themselves as a pop act), and through his industry contacts David Foster managed to persuade Barry Gibb to join them in the studio to record backing vocals with Michael. His presence was a blessing of the past on the present – and on the pop canon that Michael was re-interpreting.

Track Six was a fresh cover of a song written in 1965 by Henry Mayer, with lyrics by Johnny Mercer. 'Summer Wind' – the nostalgic tale of a fleeting romance – was made famous by Frank Sinatra, though Frank rarely played it live, making it a welcome addition to Michael's live repertoire, as this was the closest thing many people would ever get to seeing Ol' Blue Eyes perform!

'You'll Never Find Another Love Like Mine' was the album's Track Seven, a classic soul jam originally recorded by Lou Rawls in 1976. David Foster stripped the song back to its bare bones and reworked it as a slow, saccharine dance number. The song was praised for its breezy, gentle approach – quite different from the original. But, initially, Michael was dead set against including it on the album. 'David gave me the song and told me to go home and listen to it. So I was in the bath and I put it on and I said to myself, "What the hell is this?" I thought, "David Foster is nuts!" When we got into the studio he said, "In my head I can hear what it is going to sound like as a finished product and you're going to love it." I thought, "I can't argue with David Foster, since he's probably right!"' It ended up being one of Michael's favourite tunes on the album.

Track Eight was one of Queen's most famous songs, 'Crazy Little Thing Called Love', written by Freddie Mercury in 1979. Although slightly different from the rest of the songs covered on the album, after it was given the full swing treatment by Michael and David in the studio, the song would suddenly appeal to a whole new generation of music lovers.

Track Nine on the album was 'Put Your Head On My Shoulder'. This was a classic love song written by Paul Anka himself. Paul was responsible for many famous lounge and jazz classics (including one of Sinatra's biggest hits, 'My Way'). While recording this song, Michael thought about one of his first crushes at school, and imagined he was singing it to her.

'Sway', Track Ten on the album, was made famous by Dean Martin in 1954, but the song was in fact written in 1953 by a Mexican composer called Pablo Beltrán Ruiz. Before Michael's swinging mambo version of the song, it had been covered by artists from Julie London to the Pussycat Dolls. Even Björk had done

a version of the song, translated into Icelandic. As well known as the song was, Michael's romantic take on 'Sway' was a perfect addition to the album.

Track Eleven on the album was 'The Way You Look Tonight', a song written by Jerome Kern and performed by Fred Astaire in the film *Swing Time*. The song won an Academy Award in 1936 for Best Original Song, and Michael was well acquainted with it, having sung it on stage while touring with *Forever Swing*. Michael and David reworked the song with a slow, Latin rhythm.

Track Twelve on the album was a song that Michael and David discussed at length –'Come Fly With Me', made famous by Frank Sinatra in 1957. It was

one of Sinatra's all-time best-known hits, and a key part of his live performances. But it was to become a point of contention between David and his young
charge: David wanted to use the original arrangement so that the song would be
familiar to listeners, but Michael wanted to reinterpret it and add a Bublé twist.
In the end, David's experience – and financial backing of the project – won out.

The last track on the album was an all-time classic that is heralded as part
of the Great American Songbook – a title given to the greatest American songs
of the twentieth century. 'That's All' was a song originally made famous by
Nat King Cole in 1953, but Michael's version was a breathy whisper over an
acoustic guitar and soaring strings, bringing the album to a gentle close.

Michael was super excited that the album was finished and very honoured
to have been able to work alongside two music industry heroes like David and
Paul Anka.

'Working with David Foster – I mean, he's got 16 Grammys … it's truly
like working with a modern-day Beethoven. When he sits down at the piano,

you're very aware that this is a brilliant master ... he's very sure of himself and he always says that compromise breeds mediocrity,' Michael said to *You*. 'If he believes strongly in something then that's it, and I'm the same way. So we butt heads sometimes but mostly it made for better work ... we come to this great collaboration. Him and Paul Anka I can count as two of my best friends.'

As for Paul, he was excited to be involved in launching the career of such a talented and aspiring artist. 'The important thing for David and I is to get this kid off, and to lean back and go, "Look how we've helped this guy. Look what we've done with it,"' Paul said. 'That comes first.'

After they had finished work on the album, David and Bev decided between them that it would be good for Michael's career to introduce him to some high-profile music managers. But at nearly every meeting Michael went to, the first question he was asked was: 'So, when can we get rid of this Beverly?' For all his faults, Michael had been brought up to be loyal and never to turn his back on a friend. So at meeting after meeting he explained that Bev had stood by him from the start and supported him when his career was really going nowhere. There was no question of his betraying her like this. None of the managers wanted to share the limelight with Bev, and Michael wouldn't budge, so the meetings ended fruitlessly.

In desperation, David talked to Bruce Allen, the Vancouver-based manager who looked after great artists like Bryan Adams and Martina McBride, explaining the situation and asking whether Bruce would be interested in meeting Michael. Bruce was unsure. 'I understand he's a great performer,' Bruce said to David. 'But I'm not quite sure what I'd do with him.' Although it was the same worry that David had initially had about Michael, by now he was so sure of him that he wouldn't accept no for an answer. 'We've made a record to put the romance back into pop music!' he said.

Bruce was so intrigued that he asked to hear the record, and when he did, he realised it was solid gold. Bruce was impressed when he heard about how strongly Michael had always felt about singing jazz and blues. It was one of the things that convinced Bruce to take Michael on.

Michael and Bruce met at a restaurant in Vancouver and discussed the potential of working together. As all the other managers had done, Bruce asked

Michael when they could get rid of Beverly. Once again, Michael explained his loyalty to Bev and that getting rid of her was not on the cards.

Michael later remembered the moment: 'He looked at me and he'd got a big smile on his face and said, "I'm sure glad you said that, because you barely know me and I'd hate to see what you'd do to me." I looked back at him and said, "Bruce, where do I sign?"'

Bev – who was a pragmatist as well as a driven entrepreneur – realised that in order for young Michael to take the next steps in his career, he would be better guided by someone more high-profile than she was. And so, the woman who had supported and encouraged Michael as he developed from cygnet to swan gallantly stood aside to allow Bruce to manage all of Michael's affairs.

But she and Michael were close, so she remained his business partner, and Michael had nothing but praise for her. 'Bev is one of my favourite people in the world,' he said. 'She is a kind, compassionate, and trustworthy friend. I simply would not be where I am today without her belief, her tireless effort, or her unwavering support. I've learned so much watching her conduct her business and her personal life with such a great deal of intelligence and integrity. She is a special person and I'll always be her number-one fan.'

Bev returned to Vancouver for a well-deserved career break, to spend some time with her new grandchildren, Taylor and Mikayla.

Although the album had been recorded, behind the scenes the work for David and Bruce was only just beginning. They had the material, but they had to make sure Michael was promoted in the right way so that the message of his music would get through to the public. David knew that it was imperative he had the best people working with Michael. He had convinced Bruce Allen to come on board, and his second target was a top-rate publicist called Liz Rosenberg, who counted Madonna among her clients. 'She is a heavy hitter … she is at the top of her game,' Michael told Smooth Jazz Radio, talking about his team. 'When you work with them you understand quickly why they are the best.'

With his talent secured backstage, David set to work convincing the Warner Bros. music label that they should release the album. The label considered it, but asked if Michael could change his surname to that of his grandfather – Santaga – because it sounded like Sinatra. Michael refused this suggestion point-blank.

Despite his stubbornness on this point, Warner Bros. were convinced that Michael had potential, and they agreed to sign him and release his debut album. When he called home to tell his family, he spoke to his grandpa Mitch, who was almost in tears. Michael later remembered the phone call: 'When people didn't believe in me, and when I didn't believe in me, my grandfather still did. He never had a doubt.'

David also started spreading the buzz about Michael through his industry connections, and by calling in favours from friends. He arranged for Michael to sing at exclusive music industry events, where he was heard by huge Hollywood stars like Jay Leno and Kevin Spacey, who instantly became huge fans.

Michael's gigs were also getting praise from the critics. The *New York Times* reviewed a live show, revealing that Michael was 'Playful, charming and a good storyteller, he commanded the stage on Wednesday like a natural entertainer.'

And while producer David was doing his part, new manager Bruce Allen worked his magic by persuading Michael's label Warner Bros. that they needed to make him an international priority. Michael was bursting with talent and charm, and he was funny. Bruce knew that if they could send Michael around the world and find just one true fan on each continent, they would have an international superstar in the making.

Warner Bros. were unsure about taking such a huge risk with an unknown like Michael, but Bruce was such an experienced and powerful manager he persuaded them to send Michael away to play showcases in the UK, Europe and Asia. After that, Bruce called around the Warner Bros. staff in each of the locations that Michael was due to play, increasing the hype around Michael until the staff were bursting with excitement at the prospect of his visit.

So within weeks of wrapping the album's production, Michael found himself starting a round-the-world trip. Though he didn't realise it at the time, it would be the first of many.

And although he should have been overjoyed, the trip came at a price; Michael and Debbie's relationship had always suffered its ups and downs, and before Michael set off on the trip they had a huge row and decided it was best to take a break. It was with a heavy heart and an underlying feeling of sadness that Michael boarded the plane leaving Los Angeles and headed into the great unknown.

But there was no time to be sad: as he landed in South Africa and got off the plane he was hit by the oppressive heat and the exciting prospect of a new life with no ties. Michael was a great success in South Africa, and won many new fans as he toured and played concerts and TV shows there to promote his debut album.

Michael was such a hit in South Africa that Warner Bros. decided to send him to London, a key location for emerging new artists. It was well known in the music industry that if you could crack London, you had a great chance at cracking the world; but if you failed there, you'd be lucky to find work even as a wedding singer.

Audiences in the UK loved him. Although he was just playing small talent showcases – sometimes with no more than 20 people in the room – these were tastemakers, key people in the music business who were vital to Michael's success.

Michael was 27 years old, and he was on a high. Travelling the world, performing in front of hundreds of adoring fans, he had more than his fair share of women showing an interest. And, as he later admitted, he took advantage of this on more than one occasion. 'I was like a fool. I was trying to prove to myself that I was a man or something,' and an article appeared in the press.

Although his management weren't bothered by the article, Michael wasn't very happy. 'There were a couple of quotes I didn't say and a lot of it was out of context,' he said in defence. 'It was just a bunch of boys hangin', locker room talk, and it was supposed to be off the record.'

Although the article didn't damage him professionally (any press is good press, after all), personally speaking for Michael, the timing couldn't have been worse. He and Debbie had been talking and had decided to get back together.

When the article was published, Debbie was crushed. She and Michael spent many hours talking long-distance, trying to smooth things over. Michael – genuinely heartbroken at the thought of losing Debbie – professed his love over and over, and promised her he'd been faithful the whole time they were together. Debbie believed him and took him back, and for a while, things were ironed out between them.

No sooner was Michael back on solid ground after his press trips in early 2003 than his debut album, the self-titled *Michael Bublé*, was released and he set off on tour. As Michael toured the world promoting the album, it was clear that foreign audiences were falling for his charm: in the UK, South Africa and – Michael's homeland – Canada, the album went into the Top 10. In Australia it reached number 1, and was number 33 there in the top 100 albums of the year.

In fact, Warner Bros. hadn't thought Michael would do that well at first. They expected that an unknown newcomer like Michael might sell around 50,000 copies of a debut album, which wasn't much when compared to multimillion-selling artists like Michael Jackson, Jay-Z or Beyoncé.

As the niche sound of Michael's music wasn't particularly popular in the mainstream at the time, Warner Bros. had prepared themselves to build his reputation across two or three albums before they could expect him to really hit the big time. They had no idea that, rather than waiting for the sound to become a trend and hitching Michael to its bandwagon, Michael would be the one responsible for making that music popular again and bringing it to a whole new audience, worldwide.

Just a couple of months after its release on 11 February 2003, the album had already sold one million copies worldwide, with the majority of those sales coming from Asia, Australia and Europe. Michael entertained the public and was winning hearts around the world as he toured Singapore, South Africa, the Philippines, the UK, Canada, South America, and eventually the United States. Warner Bros. were astounded at the speed of Michael's success.

He was a hit everywhere he went, thanks largely to his charismatic onstage persona, which took audience participation to new extremes as he stepped down from the stage to pose for a picture with a woman in the crowd, even though taking photos had been forbidden by the venue. At another show he reached down from the stage to take a spectator's mobile phone and sang into it. At nearly every show he invited the audience to sing along and engaged them in good-natured banter.

'It should be a party!' said Michael, when asked at a press conference why he got so involved with the crowd. 'It should be music, just me jamming along with my guys in the band, and you just happened to be drinking and hanging out with me ... We should be close. You guys should be singing along. I should be in the audience with you. We should be taking pictures of each other!'

Backed by an eight-piece band, Michael skimmed and hopped around the stage full of energy, performing swinging lounge and jazz classics effortlessly. He also added a couple of contemporary songs to his set (such as George Michael's 'Faith').

'Showmanship is more important than just singing pretty,' says Michael of his live performances. 'A lot of people can sing, but I don't see a lot of people putting on a good show. I strive to entertain.'

Although a lot of people wondered how a jazz singer could possibly be getting so much attention, Michael knew it was down to the live shows. 'We're not rock stars, we play kind of jazzy standards!' he said about his band and his show. 'But our show rocks as much as AC/DC would rock! You have to see the show to understand. This is not Frank Sinatra – it's more like Marilyn Manson ... it's a crazy show!'

Michael's rise to success continued in the UK, where he appeared on several TV programmes and played sell-out shows to an appreciative British audience, who applauded, cheered and swooned in equal measure. After exposure to millions of Brits on *GMTV* and *Parkinson*, Londoners packed out the classy Café de Paris to see what all the fuss was about – and they weren't disappointed. Michael was his usual charismatic self, and cooed at the audience.

The crowd got to their feet, whooping and cheering. Michael had them in the palm of his hand. 'I think we should skip the next song ['Fever'],' he teased. 'I'm protecting you. I do this for a living and I know it can make people horny.'

Knowing his live performances would set him apart from other artists, Michael appeared on dozens of American TV shows following the release of his album in 2003, including the popular soap *Days Of Our Lives*, *The Chris Isaak Show*, *The Sharon Osbourne Show* and *Larry King Live*, but although they all boosted sales, the album *Michael Bublé* failed to get much higher than the Top 50 in the Billboard chart.

Michael understood the difference between the music industry in the UK and America. 'The great thing about the UK is that you have people like Michael Parkinson who will really push you. You appear on *Parkinson* and everyone watches that show. It really makes a difference and he loves this type of music. In America it is a lot different, you could be the biggest thing in New York and yet nobody would know who you are anywhere else in the country.

'There is a big appetite for this type of music in America. I think that at the moment people are starting to really get switched on to this type of music. People are saying that it is okay to like this kind of music, so there are a lot more, younger, people interested.'

John Reid was head of the Warner office in London at the time when Michael first played there in 2003. John was enormously experienced in the music industry, and was surprised by how quickly the international public took Michael into their hearts. 'His personality is infectious, and we saw that he was an artist willing to travel at the drop of a hat. He would get off a plane in one country, work hard there, then get on another plane and go to another country. It's wonderful to have an artist who is ready, willing and able to do that.'

Michael was also getting recognition through other channels – three songs from his debut album appeared on the soundtrack for the 2003 romantic comedy *Down With Love*, and Michael himself appeared in the Canadian film *The Snow Walker*.

In November, he followed up the surprise success of his album with an EP of Christmas songs that featured Christmas classics 'Let It Snow, Let It Snow, Let It Snow', 'The Christmas Song', 'Grown-Up Christmas List', 'I'll Be Home For Christmas' and 'White Christmas'. Thanks to Michael's appearances on American TV, the EP gathered him swathes of new followers in the US, and the lead track from the EP reached the Top 40 in the Australian singles chart at a time of year when, ironically, the country was celebrating a sweltering summer.

By the end of the year, Michael had sold three million copies of his debut, smashing everyone's expectations. The album was a much bigger hit than anyone had anticipated. But although Michael was enjoying the partying associated with his new career, he refused to blow his first big pay-cheques on fancy cars or expensive watches. Instead, he spent the money on his parents, paying for them to go on a holiday to Vegas so that his mum could play the slot machines – a luxury pastime for her, which she had rarely been able to indulge in before.

Despite his commercial success around the world, many viewed Michael as nothing more than a gimmick – a karaoke artist who sung other people's songs, and could offer nothing more. Michael shrugged off the criticism, but he knew that his critics had a point. This was largely due to the fact that it was his first album, and really, Michael had had no choice but to defer to the experience and seniority of David Foster when it came to decisions made while recording. Because of this, there were aspects that Michael was unhappy with. The arrangements for 'Come Fly With Me' and 'For Once In My Life' had been taken directly from the originals, and Michael was disappointed that he and David Foster hadn't worked more of an original slant on them.

'I mean, by taking those songs that were arrangements that Sinatra had done, I put myself on a cross,' Michael said in an interview with *You*. 'Then everyone was gonna say, you're trying to be Sinatra. But really this was a battle I had lost to David Foster. We didn't mean to steal the song, it was meant to be a tribute to the man. But that's experience – we make mistakes and we learn from them.'

Added to this, Michael didn't want to be singing other people's songs forever. The young singer was ambitious and determined to write his own material to be added to the musical history books.

So as his whirlwind of touring and promoting his debut album in 2003 drew to a close, back at home for Christmas, Michael started planning some new songs for his second record – songs that he wanted to write himself.

# climbing the ladder to success

3

Since his debut album had been released in 2003, Michael's life had become a whirlwind of flights, hotel rooms, shows and interview after interview, tirelessly pushing his music and always with a smile on his face.

In fact, he had done so many interviews and met so many journalists that, in early 2004, when one reporter in Manila asked how he described his average day, Michael replied: 'I begin my day mostly by waking up and going and doing an interview and then doing another 27 more ... but I'm in a different country, a different city every single day or week and through the whole day I'll do press. Or I might have a show and then sleep. No parties for me. I mean, I don't want to wake up and give you stupid answers for this interview!'

Warner Bros. believed it would take time to build Michael's career, so they hadn't invested in any music videos, nor had they pushed singles from his debut to be radio hits. But the album had hit the Top 100 in 15 countries across the world, and went double platinum in his ancestral nation of Italy, triple platinum in his homeland of Canada, and quintuple platinum in Australia.

Quite a feat for a young man who just a few years previously was singing on cruise ships and dressing up as Santa to try and get a showbiz break!

To capitalise on Michael's success, the label rushed out a live DVD and CD set titled *Come Fly With Me*, which captured Michael's explosive performance on stage and was intended to keep the interest of the public until he recorded his second album proper. The CD/DVD set got to number 55 in the American chart, and was re-released due to popular demand at the end of 2004.

There was also another Michael Bublé release in 2004, though not exactly a planned one. Michael's quick rise to fame had attracted the interest of the studio that had made the film *Totally Blonde*. They decided to rush out the previously unreleased soundtrack with songs sung by him on it, renaming it *Totally Bublé* and redesigning the cover so it had a picture of Michael on it. Although Michael wasn't happy about this, as he had not explicitly agreed to the release, there was nothing he or Warner Bros. could do.

But there was little time for Michael to fret over such small things – especially when he found out that he was being honoured at the 2004 Juno Awards. The Junos, presented annually to Canadian musical artists and bands to recognise their talent and achievements, had nominated Michael in two categories: New Artist of the Year and Album of the Year. He lost out to Sam Roberts for best album, but managed to carry home the Juno Award for best new artist, an incredible achievement so early in his professional career.

Feeling invigorated by his win, Michael ploughed on across America on tour. He wowed audiences with his smart and sharp onstage look: his tousled mess of brown hair, eyes that looked like they'd seen a few late nights, his crisply pressed suit and white shirt. People were mesmerised by his deep, rich voice, and teenagers giggled as he oozed charm, flirting with everyone in the audience. His years of performing practice meant that he had a natural stage presence that made everyone feel at ease. This was the kind of star quality that couldn't be learned overnight.

On occasion, Michael's new-found celebrity status got out of control. Backstage at concerts and some after-parties, Michael had to be chaperoned by security guards, as the gaggle of adoring women was so large he was unable even to go to the bathroom without being mobbed.

When asked about his new sex-symbol status, Michael knew it was the power of being on stage that attracted women to him. 'Look, if a geeky guitarist is on stage and has all the attention, girls go crazy,' he told the *Herald Sun* when asked about his sex appeal. 'If Mick Jagger were working at Subway, do you think girls would think he's the hottest thing on the planet? No.'

But the press liked to think that the mass public adoration had started to go to Michael's head, and stories of a new rock-star attitude began breaking.

Luckily for Michael, he was forced to keep his feet on the ground by phone calls from his mum, dad and his two sisters, and, of course, his adoring grand-father Mitch. They forced Michael to remain grounded, even when it looked like the fame might be going to his head. There were a couple of occasions of 'rock star' behaviour reported in the media that caused his parents to worry about him, but a few stern phone conversations with Mum and Dad soon put a stop to that.

'I look back now and I can't believe how I was acting,' he said later to journalist Liz Vickery. 'I would try to come across as a bit of a star in my interviews and just seemed to be arrogant. Then I was on a plane and was rude to the stewardess, this was only about a month ago as well, and I suddenly thought to myself, what am I doing? That is not what I am about at all. I think that I have got to grips with it now.'

As he toured around the world, Michael phoned home regularly to check in with Mitch, but the pair of them would hardly ever talk about life on the road. Instead, Michael wanted to gossip about all the action in the Canadian ice-hockey world – a world he was desperately missing.

To check up on his grandson – and also to experience life on the road – retired plumber Mitch went on tour with Michael in mid 2004, joining the 16-city leg of the tour through Mitch's homeland of Italy. 'The schedule is just too tough!' said Mitch afterwards. 'He's a hard-working kid. My God, I can't believe how hard! I'm bragging again, but this kid hasn't changed from day one.'

The time in Italy was made easier by Mitch's presence, but Michael was going through a tough time, desperately missing Debbie. After their painful break-up the year before, Michael and Debbie had worked through their problems, got back together and were stronger than ever. But the constant touring was still making life hard for Michael. Inspired by his sadness and loneliness, Michael started writing a song for Debbie. The song would become 'Home', the lead single from his second album, *It's Time,* and the first original Bublé material to be released.

Debbie had stuck by Michael, and watched with amazement as his career suddenly exploded before her eyes. From living together in their tiny apartment back in Canada, with Debbie paying most of the bills and Michael

struggling to get by, now Michael was selling millions of records and touring the world – and having to almost fight women off with a stick. Sometimes it was hard for Debbie to adjust to Michael's new superstar lifestyle. 'It's not always easy. I have my moments. I think the lucky thing is we've known each other for so long. He's good. He makes an effort to make sure I know it's all good,' she said in an interview with *Macleans*.

Michael decided to make the ultimate effort to let Debbie know it was 'all good' between them – he decided to propose to her! Unfortunately, the proposal didn't go exactly according to plan. Michael had the ring made in Vancouver, then shipped to LA where he had arranged to pick it up from the airport. Michael got to LAX international airport, where he waited for two hours before an official came to tell him they couldn't find it. Eventually the box was returned – but without a ring in it!

In a panicked hurry, Michael called for his publicist to meet him in the hotel lobby (he was on tour in New York at the time) and arranged for another ring to be made. He also picked out some diamond earrings for Debbie. Two days later, en route to England – where he was planning to pop the question – Michael arrived at Heathrow only to find that his suitcases (which contained the new ring and the diamond earrings) had been lost in transit. Not only were they lost – the airport staff had absolutely no idea where they were.

In an interview with the *Melbourne Herald Sun*, Michael said he realised then that that a ring was nothing more than a token, and that he didn't need a ring to tell Debbie that he wanted to spend the rest of his life with her. So Michael proposed without a ring – and Debbie, overjoyed, said yes!

Debbie accompanied Michael on parts of his tour as much as she could. But for the most part he was working and so was she, so they met up whenever they could. With such busy schedules it was hard, but newly boosted by their engagement, the lovebirds were determined to make their relationship work, no matter how difficult the circumstances.

Straight after the tour, Michael was back in Malibu with David Foster, working on the songs that would make up his second album. 'I think the sessions really benefited from having come straight off the road into the studio,' he explained later. 'There may be better pop singers and jazz singers out there, but nobody has as much passion for this music as I do and I think you can hear that.'

Although it was exciting to be working on new material, Michael was also worried about matching the success of his debut. 'The second record, I knew, had to be better than the first. I knew I had to like it more,' he told *Macleans*.

Although *Michael Bublé* had been a huge commercial success, the criticisms he had received – for doing karaoke versions of classic songs – had stuck with him and niggled at the back of his mind.

'I became less and less impressed with myself,' he said. 'More than less impressed, I became disappointed in what I had done. Not that it was terrible, or that I had ripped someone off, I just thought I could have sung this record so much better.'

As Michael grew in confidence and gained more experience in the studio, for his second album, *It's Time*, it was artist Michael rather than producer David who picked the majority of the songs and decided how they would be sung, and what arrangements would be used. David's perfectionist approach of combining vocal performances wasn't a natural fit for Michael, who wanted to record each song in one take so that it had all the energy and feeling that he put into his live performances.

David Foster's home covered 23 acres in Malibu and was the perfect place to record. It was a huge estate with tennis courts, a monorail to transport guests from the swimming pool to the hillside mansion, and – last but not least – a state-of-the-art recording studio.

It was at this luxury location that Michael, along with his session musicians, plus Nelly Furtado and renowned trumpet player Chris Botti, played through new versions of the classics, as well as Bublé's co-written track 'Home', and recorded demos for the second album.

Track One was 'Feeling Good', a famous jazz standard written by Anthony Newley and Leslie Bricusse. The song had originally been performed in the 1964 musical *The Roar Of The Greasepaint – The Smell Of The Crowd*. Since then, 'Feeling Good' had a rich history of artists making it their own: Nina

'Nobody has as much passion for this music as I do and I think you can hear that'

Simone, Bobby Darin and Sammy Davis Jr had all covered it, as had contemporary artists like the Pussycat Dolls and Muse. Michael's version was horn driven, bluesy, and kicked the album off to a smouldering start.

Michael had long been a fan of songs composed by George and Ira Gershwin, and Track Two was a tribute to this love. 'A Foggy Day (In London Town)' (music by George Gershwin, lyrics by Ira) was originally sung by Fred Astaire in the film *A Damsel In Distress*. Since its original recording in 1937, the song had been famously covered by superstars like Frank Sinatra, Ella Fitzgerald, Billie Holliday and Doris Day. Michael's version was widely applauded – even the *Washington Post* described it as 'note perfect'.

Track Three was 'You Don't Know Me', originally released as a country song by Eddy Arnold in 1955, and covered by hundreds of artists since: among them, Elvis Presley, Bette Midler and Van Morrison. The most famous version of the song was a 1962 recording by Ray Charles, and Michael's gentle, lounge take on the song was a tribute to the Ray Charles version.

Track Four was an Italian pop song from the 1960s called 'Quando, Quando, Quando'. The version that appeared on *It's Time* featured special guest Nelly Furtado on backing vocals. Nelly – a fellow Canadian – was specially requested by Michael to feature on the song. 'I wanted someone young, I wanted someone who sings beautifully and I wanted someone who sells records internationally' he said. 'So I'm thinking, yeah, there are people like that everywhere. And all of a sudden I thought, Nelly Furtado!'

Although Michael was determined to get Nelly to sing with him, others weren't so sure about his choice of guest. 'I wanted to do a duet with Nelly Furtado, and I had people saying, "Oh man, why don't we get Beyoncé – like, she's really hot right now." But I want to work with someone because I think they're stunning and because I think they're great and they're gonna get what I'm doing and it's going to complement what I'm doing,' he said in an interview with *Straight*.

Track Five was the first original material to appear on a Michael Bublé album, and was also released as the lead single from *It's Time*. The song was 'Home', the track Michael had written for Debbie while he was in Italy. 'At that time I was really missing her,' Michael said later to Cameron Adams of the *Herald Sun*. 'We'd gone through a lot of troubles and got back together. I was in the shower and the words started coming to me. It was so autobiographical.' Debbie sang backing vocals and appeared in the video for 'Home'. The material that Michael had come up with in Italy had been finished off with David's daughter Amy Foster-Gillies, herself a renowned songwriter and lyricist.

One of the Beatles' most well-known and well-loved songs, 'Can't Buy Me Love', was chosen as Track Six on the album. Michael knew only too well how fervent and passionate Beatles' fans were about the Fab Four's music, and for this reason he was nervous about tampering with the original arrangement of the song. But he went with his gut instinct and added a distinctly jazzy slant to the original upbeat pop song, figuring he would just deal with any bad reviews or criticism when they happened.

Track Seven on *It's Time* was another made famous by Nat King Cole, although it has also been covered by countless other artists. 'The More I See You' was originally written in 1945 for the musical *The Diamond Horseshoe*, starring Betty Grable and Dick Haymes (who sang 'The More I See You' in the film). Michael's big-band version matched his powerful Sinatra-esque delivery with a bright horn section, and the result was a big hit with the critics.

Track Eight was 'Save The Last Dance For Me', originally a hit for Ben E. King and the Drifters in 1960. The song enjoyed a resurgence of popularity in the 1980s, when Dolly Parton did a country cover version that appeared on her album *The Great Pretender*. A slow-paced love song, Michael's version of 'Save The Last Dance For Me' was designed to ensure there wouldn't be a dry eye left in the house by the time he'd finished singing. It was scheduled to be the second single released from *It's Time*.

'Try A Little Tenderness' was chosen to be Track Nine on the album. Composed in 1932, within a year there were three versions of the song – from the Ray Noble Orchestra, Ruth Etting and Bing Crosby. However, one of the most popular versions of the song to this day was performed by Otis Redding, transforming it from jazz standard to a soul hit. In turn, the new arrangement on *It's Time* set Michael's gentle vocals against a delicate piano, creating a new classic.

Track Ten on the album was a 1964 Motown hit by the songwriting team of Lamont Dozier and brothers Brian and Edward Holland (Jr): 'How Sweet It Is To Be Loved By You'. Originally recorded by Marvin Gaye, one of Motown's greats, the most famous cover version of the song was sung by James Taylor in 1975, with Carly Simon on harmony vocals. Already hugely popular, the song enjoyed a fresh injection of emotion as Michael asked Debbie to sit in the studio and sang the song directly to her.

Michael's approach to recording the album was to allow his emotions to drive his performances – hence requesting Debbie to be in the studio so that he could sing to her – and he did this again for Track Eleven, 'A Song for You'. Originally written and performed by Leon Russell in 1970, the song was covered by numerous other performers, including Andy Williams – one of Michael's heroes – in 1971.

Michael had already begun standing his ground with David Foster about the way the album was put together, insisting that songs were recorded in one take rather than piecing his vocals together afterwards, as David had done on *Michael Bublé*. But the pair clashed over the recording of Track Twelve, the Sinatra classic 'I've Got You Under My Skin'. Eventually David gave in to

Michael, allowing him to flex a little more muscle over the creative direction of the album.

The last song on the album, 'You And I', was written by Stevie Wonder and originally featured on his 1972 album *Talking Book*. A slow-paced love song, with its soaring strings and sad piano, 'You And I' turned out to be one of the most intimate moments on *It's Time*.

Unlike his debut album, *It's Time* featured no modern classics, though Michael had wanted to cover Lenny Kravitz's 'Stand By My Woman' and 'Black Hole Sun' by Soundgarden, even though he didn't feel that they fitted the style of the album. 'Hopefully I'll have another ten, twenty records to fit all these songs in!' he said while going through the final tracklisting.

The year 2004 drew to a close, and Michael grew nervous about the release of his second album. His celebrity success had him in a constant churn – he was petrified it would disappear as suddenly as it had come. There were many moments that made it worthwhile for him, though, like giving extravagant gifts for Christmas that year: getting a car for his mum, an antique watch for his dad, and giving his sisters $30,000 each. 'They were the moments I thought, okay, this is why I'm doing this. I've got to share it,' Michael explained.

But as the bells rang in the new year of 2005, Michael shook off those feelings of self-doubt and allowed himself to enjoy his success. The love of his life had agreed to be his wife, he had a wonderful family who loved him unconditionally and he was about to unleash his second album on the world. Once again, he fell asleep at nights praying it would be a success.

# releasing *it's time*

A s 8 February 2005 approached, Michael was nervous. It was a big day for him – the date that his second album, *It's Time,* was due for release as a download on iTunes.

But all the sleepless nights were for nothing. Critics loved *It's Time* and were more generous than they had been about his debut, *Michael Bublé*. The Beatles' cover that he had been so nervous about, 'Can't Buy Me Love', was in actual fact singled out for praise by several jazz critics.

Although Michel had been proud of his first album, he was bursting with pride when he spoke about *It's Time*. 'On the first record it was easier for me to sell it commercially because it was more schlocky, and schlock sells,' he said in an interview with the *Herald Sun*. 'But every time I talked to a journalist or a critic, I'd sit down and they'd say, 'So, what do you think of your record?' I didn't think it was a horrible record by any means. I knew why people liked it. But it was easier this time because I believe in this record,' he said.

Michael's faith in his second album was well placed. It reached number 1 in Canada, Japan and Italy, and made it into the Top 10 in America, Australia, the UK, Switzerland, Austria, Sweden and Norway. In fact, *It's Time* would go on to spend a total of 104 weeks on the American Billboard Jazz Chart

(and was awarded Top Jazz Album of the Year in the same chart, as well as top spot in the Australian End of Year Jazz & Blues Chart).

As soon as *It's Time* came out, Michael immediately hit the road on tour. His tireless attitude towards his work was born out of a conversation he had with one of his all-time heroes, singer Tony Bennett. Born in New York in 1926, Tony had started singing at a young age, but was drafted into the army in his late teens. Once released from active duty, Tony embarked on a career as a crooner, singing pop and jazz classics in the 1950s. His career hit a high in the 1960s, but he fell out of favour in the 1970s. He managed a remarkable career comeback in the 1980s and 1990s, and he knew the importance of working hard.

After Tony's first real hit, the singer – lulled into a false sense of career security – had celebrated by forgetting about work and going on holiday. 'I was lackadaisical and I didn't have another number-1 hit for five or six years. Never again did I get complacent,' Tony told Michael.

It was sage advice and Michael took it to heart and never once complained about his hectic tour schedule or how gruelling it was to be constantly on the road, on the move. Gwen Stefani's album *Love. Angel. Music. Baby.* had come out at the end of 2004, and Gwen was also on tour in 2005; Michael spotted her on many of the planes he took around the world, as they both travelled around promoting their albums. 'I sat with this woman on 16 different airplanes. Never spoke to her, never met her. I was busting my gut, doing all this promo, and so was she. And look at her success,' Michael said to Sydney's *Herald Sun*.

'People wonder why records don't work – Gwen Stefani was up for the challenge. She was probably tired and grumpy, but you can't just make a record these days and hope the radio will play it and do all the work for you. It's not going to happen.'

But just as Michael liked to work hard, there was another side to him shown in the press – the side that liked to play hard. In reality, though, the party never lasted long. 'I can't party,' Michael said to the *Edmonton Sun*. 'I can party for five minutes. I've never been a big drinker. But hey, I work too much. I don't get a chance to party.' So maybe it was because he wasn't accustomed to drinking, or perhaps some dodgy food was to blame, when

Michael suffered an unfortunate incident at a party at Hollywood A-lister Leonardo DiCaprio's house. After enjoying some tacos and cocktails and chatting with others, Michael suddenly felt ill.

Michael's dry sense of humour about the incident was misinterpreted by the media, and the event ended up being portrayed as a decadent night of heavy drinking and debauchery. Following some media reports, one of the publicists working for manager Bruce Allen called Michael into the office, stating her concern about Michael's loose tongue. She offered Michael some training on how to answer interview questions and handle the media.

'I said, no, I'm not going to do that,' Michael told the *Edmonton Sun*. 'Even my mother will call me and say, "Can't you just be nice?" I *am* nice, Ma! What's the worst thing that people have said about me? I've smoked pot. I've slept with some people. I didn't hurt anyone. I didn't rape anyone. I didn't take any hard drugs. I'm just being a normal person.'

Often, it was impossible to tell whether Michael was serious or joking. His dry sense of humour didn't translate well onto paper. But in person, his rakish

charm and a flash of his smile soon reassured you of his intentions.

His publicist and manager rolled their eyes upon reading about Michael's hard-partying lifestyle. Meanwhile, Michael boarded a plane from Los Angeles, bound for Sydney, Australia.

Michael had been popular in Australia ever since his debut album came out. The Australians had warmed to the crooner faster than any other country in the world, and there was media hysteria about his mini tour in April 2005. As a result, *It's Time* was certified platinum there just two weeks after its release. While Michael was touring the country in April, tickets went on sale for a September/October tour. Though the tour was months away, five consecutive shows at the Sydney Opera House sold out within days.

While Michael was undertaking his mini tour of Australia in May, he was invited to the Logies – the Australian television industry awards ceremony. Backstage at the awards, Michael was introduced to some key figures in the Australian TV industry, nearly all of whom were huge fans of his and who gushed over how much they loved his recent album release.

Through the throngs of people that he was introduced to, Michael met one woman whose beauty left him breathless. Michael mistakenly thought she was a producer for the BBC. He didn't realise that she was actually British actress Emily Blunt. As they shook hands, Michael thought to himself how cute she was. But this was a new Michael, dedicated to his fiancée Debbie. As Emily walked away, he vowed that he would not think about her again.

Luckily for Michael, he had more than enough on his plate to keep him occupied as he tirelessly toured and promoted *It's Time*. He was invited to do interview after interview, in one country after another, all around the world. The question he was asked repeatedly in almost every interview was why he thought the music he was singing held such universal appeal for people. On his travels around the world he had the chance to watch audiences interact with the music he loved so much. He saw it improve moods and lift spirits, heal wounds and change lives.

'I think people feel like the world is going to shit. That doesn't sound like a really eloquent way of saying it, but you turn on the news, it's scary. I think people really feel the need to escape that,' he said in an interview with *Macleans*.

Regardless of what was popular in the charts at any particular time, Michael felt there was an all-time, enduring charm to the music he loved. It didn't matter to him whether a song was written in 1930 by George Gershwin, or in 1991 by George Michael. For Michael, as long as a song had a beautiful melody, nice lyrics and a great beat, then to him it was a timeless classic.

Michael had seen music transcend the borders of countries, enjoyed by people of all cultures. He knew he must be one of the luckiest men in the world – to be living his lifelong dream of touring the world, playing to thousands of adoring fans on every continent. The travelling had been a particular thrill for Michael, who before his early twenties had never even left North America. But these days, it was rare for him to be back there for more than a week at a time.

In mid 2005, Michael managed to squeeze in some dates in the United States, much to the joy of American audiences. His years of experience had led to an onstage confidence that couldn't be imitated. Michael enjoyed adlibbing, and made off-the-cuff jokes with his audience. He was so confident that he commanded the stage, both when he was singing and when he was chatting to the crowd. Michael put so much into every show, frequently jumping off the stage and skipping about the audience, high-fiving people and encouraging them to sing along with him. With his impressive vocal pipes, Michael would also frequently abandon his microphone and sing without any kind of amplification; he could still be heard clearly in venues of almost any size.

As part of the mini tour through America, one of Michael's concerts at the Wiltern Theatre in Los Angeles was filmed, with a view to releasing it in November of that year as a live CD and DVD titled *Caught In The Act*. The show was trademark Michael: him performing alongside a powerful 27-piece band, singing classics from his two albums: from 'Try A Little Tenderness' and 'I've Got You Under My Skin' to 'Sway' and 'Save The Last Dance for Me'.

The famous Italian popstrel Laura Pausini appeared on stage with Michael as a little bonus act, giving her vocals to a duet of 'You'll Never Find Another Love', and other guests on the show were Chris Botti and Michael's pal, singer Josh Groban. As was customary with most of Michael's gigs, by the end of the show the crowd was dancing in the aisles.

The shows in America gave Michael some long-overdue time with fiancée Debbie. The pair enjoyed a few dinner dates in downtown LA, where they ate fine food and tried to reignite the romance that was suffering due to their increasingly busy diaries. Though they had become engaged just a matter of happy months before, Michael's gruelling travelling schedule left little time for the lovebirds to spend any quality time together.

The couple's incompatible work schedules were driving a wedge between them. But Michael – who had wanted success so desperately for so long – could not say no to his work, and that meant staying out on the road. Debbie was keen to pursue her own career and was unwilling to give up her dreams to follow Michael. As he told *The Telegraph*, 'I was working. She was working. It got to be that we were never together.' It was a terrible situation for the two of them, who had been a couple for such a long time. Debbie understood the call of fame for Michael and was supportive of his lifestyle, but Michael couldn't help but feel awful every time he had to board a plane to leave the country – and her – behind.

'Debbie never made me feel guilty, I just did feel guilty,' he said to the *Herald Sun*. 'How can you say to someone "I love you very much but my priority is my career right now. If I don't do this now I'll kick myself for the rest of my life"?' He and Debbie spent fretful hours discussing their relationship, trying to work out how they could solve the problems that were caused by spending so much time apart. Unfortunately, there was to be no happy ending to the story. With tears in their eyes, Michael and Debbie had the final discussions about their relationship.

It was decided. Their relationship was over.

Michael was distracted as he travelled though Australia, Singapore, the Philippines and Thailand, playing to arenas full of thousands of adoring fans.

He turned to music as his salvation. In the hotel rooms that became home while he was on tour, Michael started writing a song called 'Lost', that he intended as an anthem for love that didn't work out. It was 'a song for relationships that end but you don't want to discard the person you obviously still care for,' he told the *Herald Sun*. 'Just because you're not together doesn't mean you won't love them forever.'

In the chic and modern surroundings of Melbourne's Como Hotel, Michael started putting down lyrics on paper. But in the end the whole process was so painful that he had to put away what he had worked on to concentrate on his live shows. Michael wanted to give his fans the best night's entertainment they'd ever had in their lives; whatever personal issues he was going through had to be left at the side of the stage.

But as one door closes, another one opens. And as Michael was healing from the wounds of his ended relationship, he had a chance encounter at one of his shows, when he bumped into none other than the British actress he had met earlier in the year at the Logies, Emily Blunt, who was backstage with a large group of industry acquaintances. Michael still didn't realise that Emily – a relative unknown at the time – was an actress, and thought she was a producer for the BBC. Emily had seen the concert and had thought Michael was great; they got chatting and she mentioned that she was an actress.

'I thought, "Right, like every other person waiting on table...!"' admitted Michael later. But he and Emily had a rapport, and stayed in touch after the concert. As both of them had just come out of long-term relationships, they took their time about getting to know each other. But Michael's interest had been caught enough for him to seek out *My Summer Of Love*, a critically acclaimed British film released in 2004 about an ill-fated teenage lesbian love affair, in which Emily had starred. 'To say that I was blown away would be an understatement,' Michael said. 'I was like, "But you're brilliant!"'

Although Michael and Emily were taking things slowly and getting to know each other, Michael was advised by his manager Bruce and publicist Liz that, given his new, superstar status, it would be prudent to find some way of releasing the news of his breakup with Debbie to his fans and the media.

Michael spent days with Bruce and Liz composing statement after statement, trying to find the right words. He arrived in the UK at the end of October 2005 for a string of dates, and decided the time was right to release the information.

'Debbie and I have mutually decided to end our engagement,' Michael said, in a short statement put on his website on 2 November. 'I will always have a very special place in my heart for her and hope she feels the same way. I cherish the many memories and hope that we remain good friends for the rest of our lives. She truly is a beautiful person inside and out. There's no big story to tell here and during this emotional time for us both and out of respect for me and for Debbie and our families, I would so appreciate there not being speculation and conversations about this subject. It's really personal and just between Debbie and I. Thank you all for your sensitivity about the situation.'

Michael did not let the changes to his personal life affect his performances on stage. He played to thousands of people in stadiums across the UK: in Dublin, Edinburgh, Manchester, Birmingham, London, and more; and then across Europe in Holland, France, Italy, Germany and Spain before the end of the year.

At a press conference kicking off the Italian tour dates, Michael proudly displayed a new Italian passport, which set in stone his Italian heritage from grandfather Mitch, who had lived in the small Italian village of Preganziol before emigrating to Canada.

Although Michael put everything into each performance, the shows were tinged with sadness when it was time to play 'Home'. The song had been Michael's first original single and was a huge hit, so there was no chance of leaving it out of any performance. But every time Michael sang it, he had to relive the memories of his newly ended relationship with Debbie, night after night.

'At first it was weird,' Michael said to the *Herald Sun*. 'It was really tough and emotional. It's a very autobiographical song. It was art imitating life imitating art.'

Although 2005 ended with the sadness of his ended relationship with Debbie, it certainly wasn't all bad. He had a new love interest in rising-star actress Emily Blunt, and though the couple had only been dating for a few weeks, Michael's pangs over losing Debbie were mixed with the excitement of a budding new relationship. Even though he had been on tour almost constantly since *It's Time* was released, Michael was living his dream, and he wouldn't let himself forget that, stating: 'I wouldn't have traded any amount of domestic bliss for the experience of performing before Prince Charles at the Royal Variety Show or selling out Sydney Opera House five nights running.'

He found cause for celebration as his album *It's Time* celebrated a huge second anniversary in the charts in February 2006. It had spent a total of 104 weeks on the Billboard's Top Jazz Albums Chart, where it remained at the number-1 spot for a record 78 weeks, breaking the all-time record for the highest number of weeks at number 1 by any artist.

As the studio arranged a small party to celebrate Michael's achievement, there was even more good news when adding up the total sales figures. *It's Time* had gone platinum in no fewer than 14 countries, including the UK, Holland, Austria, Germany, Sweden, France, Belgium, Switzerland, Ireland, Indonesia, South Africa and the Philippines. In Michael's homeland of Canada the album had gone platinum six times, whilst in Australia it had gone quadruple platinum, and in Singapore and America it had gone double platinum.

The celebration was echoed with news that *It's Time* had been nominated for a Grammy in the category of Best Traditional Pop Vocal Album. Beaming with delight, Michael posed for photographs on the red carpet with one of his all-time heroes, Tony Bennett. Although he didn't win the Grammy, the awards ceremony was a good warm-up for the 2006 Juno Awards.

As Michael pulled up to the grand Halifax Metro Centre in Nova Scotia, he had a surprise in store for the awaiting paparazzi. Michael was accompanied by his new girlfriend, Emily Blunt. 'I tried to move slow because we'd both just come through break-ups, but the truth is I was pretty much instantly infatuated,' Michael told the *Sunday Times*. 'I mean, forgetting for a moment how beautiful she is, she's got this wonderful personality.'

Emily, along with the rest of Michael's entourage at the Junos, jumped to her feet and clapped with delight when Michael was called to the stage to accept three awards: Artist of the Year, Album of the Year for *It's Time*, and Single of the Year for 'Home'. The previous night, at a Juno Awards Dinner, Michael had been presented with an award for Pop Album of The Year for *It's Time*, bringing his grand total to four awards.

The year had got off to a fabulous start, both in his private life and professionally. And things were set to stay that way for some time to come.

# finding love again

N ever one to rest on his laurels, Michael spent the majority of 2006 on the road, with a hectic schedule of dates that had him scheduled to visit 46 countries within a 12-month period. There were few artists who could create the same kind of atmosphere at a live show as Michael could, and he knew that in order to make sure he was around for years to come, his career had to be organised around live shows.

Although the endless drag of flights and faceless hotel rooms had been difficult when he was promoting his debut album, with his increased popularity (and increased investment from the label), Michael's touring entourage also increased, often including members of his family – anyone who was free at the time: his parents, grandparents, sisters – which made the touring adventure more of a home away from home experience.

'It means much more to me seeing how thrilling it is for them, especially my grandpa,' Michael said in an interview with the *Sunday Times*. 'They think it's the greatest thing, having a late breakfast then a stroll around whichever new city we're in. Later on there'll be some dinner in advance of the show and they'll start having a few pops. In fact, I doubt if they're totally sober at any point, but they don't need to be. They're on holiday.'

Michael's hectic schedule was – for once – equally matched by that of his girlfriend. Emily had worked on two films that were released in 2006 – a thriller called *Irresistible,* starring Susan Sarandon and Sam Neill, and romantic comedy *The Devil Wears Prada.* Emily played the assistant of ice-queen fashion-magazine editor Meryl Streep, vying for her boss's favour against new assistant Anne Hathaway.

Though the film was packed with stars, it was Emily who stood out, as the neurotic and anxious assistant of the same name who teeters through the film on the edge of a nervous breakdown. As Michael and Emily attended the premiere of the film, Michael sat in awe of his girlfriend. 'Kiddo, you stole the entire movie. Your life is never going to be the same again!' he whispered to her as the credits rolled and everyone in the theatre got to their feet, applauding.

'I'd much rather go to a movie,
eat some sushi and have some wine
than go to the party of the year'

The couple had fallen deeply in love with each other. Michael bought a million-dollar home in Vancouver, which was intended to be a home for him and Emily whenever they were in the country and not working. And though their public life was full of red carpets, award shows and glamorous photo shoots, in reality Michael and Emily were both homely people who preferred the intimacy of staying at home to chasing celebrity parties around Hollywood.

Michael shared his love of ice hockey with Emily, who quickly became a fan, and they rode around Vancouver on Michael's beloved purple Vespa. 'I'd much rather go to a movie, eat some sushi and have some wine than go to the party of the year,' Michael said about his love for home comforts. 'Honestly, I wish the awards shows could bring the camera to my house instead.'

And considering how nice Michael's pad was, no wonder. Journalist Craig McLean, writing for the *Telegraph*, gave outsiders a rare peep: 'There are many other rooms in which to hang out in this property sitting on 15,543 square feet of land: the room with the giant television; the room with the piano and bar; the basement room with the table-tennis, air-hockey game, darts board, mini-cinema, elephant-sized easy chairs and second bar (backed by a wall-mounted waterfall). Tonight, we … will also spend much time on the heated patio, with its views over the swimming pool, Burrard Inlet and Bryan Adams' old place.'

In those rare moments at home, they behaved as if they were any normal couple. Michael would do chores around the place like changing light bulbs and taking out the trash. The couple would play board games – their favourite was Scrabble. But in reality, both Michael and Emily found themselves increasingly in the spotlight of media attention, he for his music, and she for her movies.

Even so, Michael maintained that he and Emily preferred the quiet life. 'I'm not in the tabloids,' he was quoted as saying in Rush and Molloy's celeb gossip column in the *New York Times*. 'We don't live that lifestyle. Never in the tabloids. Look – I hate Hollywood parties, and I hate most other celebrities, to be really honest with you.'

'We're not exactly Brad and Angelina,' Emily added. 'Nobody really knows who I am, especially in Canada, and Michael doesn't court publicity. We're both outsiders really.'

The reality was that Michael just didn't have the time for Hollywood parties. Mindful of the advice of his hero, Tony

Bennett, he spent most of his time on the road, going from city to city, concert to concert. Emily, who had a little more time off than Michael between film shoots, took advantage of her schedule and joined Michael and his musicians on their tour bus for some dates across America.

Contrary to what some people might have thought about Michael, given the kind of music he loved, the tour bus was itself a bit of a party zone. Michael and his band drank whiskey, smoked cigars and played cards, and their language could be quite unsavoury. 'I've become quite unshockable on the bus. Michael and his band, they're just all quite lewd, the way they talk about people, but the funniest thing is the fans,' said Emily about her time on tour. 'I've been bodyslammed off the bus as they try to get to him!'

While Emily was able to join Michael on tour for some of 2006, her star went into orbit after *The Devil Wears Prada* was released, and job offers started coming thick and fast. Michael was overjoyed: the guilt he had felt whilst with Debbie was relieved by the knowledge that Emily was as dedicated to her career as he was to his.

Michael explained their arrangement further: 'It's easier, in that I can leave her in LA, I had to go to work in Vancouver and she goes, "Okay, I've got to go to work in Albuquerque." There's no guilt. Emily gets it. When she goes away, not only do I give her no chance to feel guilt, I'll go: "This is great, this film will be great for you." We pump each other up. There's definitely a cohesive understanding. It's nice.'

Michael even got to play the supporting-partner role as he accompanied Emily to the January 2007 Golden Globe Awards in Hollywood, where Emily was nominated for a Golden Globe for her role in the Hollywood smash *The Devil Wears Prada*. Although she didn't win for that, she was also nominated for her role in *Gideon's Daughter* (made by independent producer TalkbackThames), for which she did win!

Michael couldn't have been more overjoyed: 'It was the greatest night of my career,' he told *People*. 'She was so humble, and I was so emotional. I kept shaking her, saying "Don't you know what's just happened?!" I really have an issue with enjoying the moment, and for the first time I understood how it felt to allow yourself to be so happy and pumped.'

For Michael, it was a chance to experience the joy that his family felt when they saw him doing so well. 'I understood what my mum and dad and grand-parents say when they tell me they get more joy out of seeing me succeed than I do,' he said. 'It was like an epiphany. I was so full of pride, it's overwhelming to see a person you love do well.'

Although the awards ceremony had been a complete high for them, Michael found himself in trouble for some comments he had made – completely tongue-in-cheek – to an *Associated Press* reporter on the red carpet. 'Everybody's congratulating her on her two nominations but nobody seems to realise that I was nominated as well: shiniest shoes,' Michael said. 'Clooney is always my biggest competition.'

Michael's dry sense of humour would get him into more trouble just a couple of days later, when he was interviewed by the Canadian Press about the upcoming 2007 Grammy Awards. Michael was nominated for his CD/DVD set *Caught In The Act*, but he said he would be boycotting the February event in Los Angeles because the category he was nominated in – Best Traditional Pop Vocal Album – wasn't scheduled to be presented live on TV.

'Our category is selling way too many records to be given away at a dinner before, so I'm just not going to show up,' Michael said to the *Canadian Press*. 'Why should I go to the Grammys? I'll lose. No, I'll lose. They might as well have already scratched Tony Bennett's name into the damn thing. I'm not going.' Instead, Michael insisted he would prefer to stay home and watch his favourite hockey team, the Canucks.

It was an off-the-cuff remark that Michael said without thinking. Within a matter of hours, those words had been turned into a 'Bublé snubs Grammys' tidal wave that washed over news and celebrity sites on the internet. Michael was horrified that a comment so flippant could become worldwide news in a matter of hours. He was worried – so worried that he felt physically sick, as if someone had punched him in the stomach. After a stern ticking off from his publicist, Michael acknowledged 'I should, by now, be a little more tactful about the words I choose to say.'

To try and quell the storm, Michael's publicist hastily arranged an interview with *Sun Media*, so that Michael could explain and retract his initially harsh comments. 'I don't think I'm going, but it's not because they're not televising the award,' he said. 'It depends on how much work I have to do on the record. But it is an honour.

'One thing that people will get to know about me is I basically say how I feel,' Michael continued. 'I have a hard time filtering, but I think I could have been far more eloquent in what I said earlier. I was just trying to be funny and I don't think it turned out very funny. I really would hate for those people that honoured me with that nomination to think that I'm too big for my britches and I'm going, "Yeah, screw that." I would never want to disrespect that award. I surely do not want to come off as some egotistical ass.'

Michael stated that his not going had nothing to do with the fact that his category wouldn't be broadcast on TV, and insisted he wasn't boycotting the Grammys – rather, that he would be busy doing press in Vancouver on that day.

Michael's publicist, who was well versed at directing this kind of media crisis, told Michael that regardless of what he'd intended to say, if he didn't attend the Grammys then it would be viewed as a snub. Michael, who was keen to win a Grammy one day, realised that he would have to do a U-turn on his initial stance and attend the ceremony.

To get some breathing space from the press, Michael's publicist told him to stay home and try to relax for a couple of days. Michael paced around his Vancouver home with the curtains drawn, but he was struck by some wisdom offered to him by one of his managers. 'She said, "For all the wonderful things that have happened in your life, and all the wonderful things you have, you do know that fame is the worst of all."' Michael – the young boy who had slept with the Bible under his pillow, praying for fame – thought about the old proverb, 'Be Careful What You Wish For…', and realised quite how true it really was.

A spokesperson from Warner Music Canada issued a statement to the press, saying that Michael had realised he had an opening in his schedule on the night of the Grammys, so he would be attending after all.

The event itself was a fairly quiet event, as far as Michael's attendance went. He kept his mouth shut on the red carpet, passing pleasantries with journalists and other attendees, but he had been well and truly burned.

'It was devastating. I'm not exaggerating, I shook for two days,' Michael said later to the *Herald Sun*. 'But if I could go back, I'd have said the exact same thing, just not in such an ineloquent way. This thing will haunt me for the next twenty years. But what the hell … Put it in context. I just said rap, R&B and rock all get their chance to get shown on the Grammys, how could this music not? I embarrassed myself by using the words I used.'

The mass media interest was testament to just how famous Michael had become. A year ago, no one had paid much attention to anything he said – flippant comments weren't reported, and jokes with reporters remained off the record. But after the enormous success of his second album – and with his new, hot, media girlfriend – Michael was suddenly big news. The press was interested in everything he had to say – and unforgiving in how they reported it.

It slowly dawned on Michael that perhaps some lessons in learning to deal with the media might not be such a bad thing. In an interview with *AP*, Michael admitted the biggest mistakes of his career had been caused by his big mouth. 'I am a candid interview and I have a dark and dry sense of humor – a very Canadian sense of humor and I am only learning now, stupidly, that you can't read tongue. When I say something funny in a newspaper and I meant it to be funny, it doesn't read that way. It is the same if you have ever gotten an e-mail and you think, "What did I ever do to make this person respond this way?" They never meant to be aggressive, but you can't read the tone. I've said things. There were comments about many things I wish I would have said in a different way or a more eloquent way.'

Suddenly, there was no avoiding Michael – the swing singer was everywhere you turned. His version of 'Come Fly With Me' was used in an advert by Starbucks, and ESPN used 'Feeling Good' to soundtrack their poker coverage. Michael's star was shining so brightly he was even asked to sing at the $6 million wedding of Australian media tycoon James Packer, rubbing shoulders at the event with Tom Cruise and Katie Holmes, John Travolta and Rupert Murdoch.

For Christmas in 2006, Michael had given his parents $1 million, and given his two sisters $50,000 each – signal enough that his lifelong career ambitions were starting to pay off. And his generosity extended beyond his nearest and dearest: as his tour came to an end, he paid for 45 members of his hardworking band, crew, and the secretaries from his management office in Vancouver to have a five-day Hawaiian holiday.

But all this fame came at a price, including several phone calls from his mother telling him to watch his mouth the next time he was talking to the press. Having learned his lesson the hard way, Michael retreated into the studio to put the finishing touches to his third album.

# *call me irresponsible* 6

Escaping from the pressures of the media, Michael had music on his mind – specifically, the song he had started writing when he and Debbie split up; the one he'd had to put away. He revisited the lyrics, and called on Canadian songwriter Jann Arden to help him finish the track, which he had called 'Lost': an anthem for love lost, and ended relationships. Jann helped Michael add an uplifting aspect to the song. After the song had been written, Michael called Debbie and played the song to her. Moved to tears, Debbie bawled her eyes out. 'It was a tribute to us,' said Michael. 'Sometimes relationships don't work out because love isn't enough, but that doesn't mean you have to discard the person. There is a way to end a relationship and still be there when they need you. That's basically what it's about.'

Some thought it was a strange gesture for Michael to write a song about an ex-girlfriend, while he was happily in love with his current squeeze. But Michael had feelings about Debbie that needed to be settled, and the only way to do that was through music.

'I was working. She was working. It got to be that we were never together and so we grew apart. Facing up to that was pretty crushing for both of us,' he said later about his break-up with Debbie and the origins of the song 'Lost'.

'And the fact is I love her still, as much as I ever did. You don't just write

someone out of your life when they've meant so much to you,' he went on. 'There'll always be a loyalty there. Yes, I'm in love again and have this beautiful girl who I'm mad for. But there remains a place in my heart for Debbie and I'd be there for her if ever the chips were down. Emily understands that, luckily, and cares similarly about guys with whom she has been involved in the past.'

In fact, things with Emily were going so well that Michael had taken the plunge and flown to England to meet her family. The couple were dividing their spare time between Michael's place in Vancouver and Emily's place in London, and it was on one of these trips that the journey was extended to the Home Counties, to meet the Blunts. 'Because I was very quickly so crazy about Emily it felt like there was a lot riding on how it went when I first met her parents,' said Michael in an interview with the *Sunday Times*.

Michael was super nervous when he walked up the steps to the Blunt family home, but the door was opened by Emily's younger brother, who enveloped Michael in a big hug, and Michael knew everything was going to be okay. 'Her dad is just great – he's teaching me cricket,' Michael said, of the first meeting. 'And her mum? We sat down to eat, and talking to me she was so dry, so British and just so great. The great thing is I can be myself with them – be rude, swear, whatever – and they just laugh.'

He went on: 'My ex's parents are sweet and lovely but also very proper. I had to be on my best behaviour and couldn't always manage it. Emily's just accept me as the person I am and seem to like me for it. It's such a big, big relief.'

And Emily couldn't have been happier. She had been accepted with open arms into the Bublé clan – Michael's family were as much in love with the British actress as Michael was himself. And Michael was just the kind of down-to-earth guy she liked. 'He's a fart in a bottle,' she told the *Sunday Times*. 'There's very little dancing, candlelight and flowers, just lots of stay-at-home nights

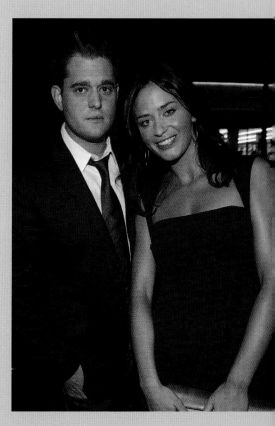

watching the Canucks and playing video games. It's all right. I like a boy with food down his shirt.'

Luckily for Michael, Emily also had a sense of humour and understood when he let his mouth run away with him. In April 2007, while Michael was being interviewed, he ended up accidentally proposing to her: 'I really feel like, you know, I'm going to marry her … I want to be the dad of her kids. I haven't proposed to her yet. But I will do that. In a way I'm sort of proposing to her through this interview!' The news of the pseudo-proposal tore across the gossip sites, but afterwards both Emily and Michael remained tight-lipped about the whole incident. Shortly after, Michael was on the receiving end of another ticking off on the phone from his mother.

'Me being dry, I realise now I can't even joke about stuff because they've used it to sell their magazine,' Michael told *AP* about his apparent 'proposal' in *Hello*. 'They have taken it completely out of context. Now I see it in newspapers at home and throughout the States. I see that I have been engaged to Emily without ever asking her. The big question I had was, do you think I would ask her to marry me through *Hello* magazine? Would I do something like that? Would she allow that to happen? It is completely ridiculous.'

But there was definitely support in the Bublé camp for the union, mostly from Michael's mum, Amber. 'I love her,' she told *People*. 'In fact if he doesn't marry her, I'll kill him. But we'd find someone in the family to marry her because we're not letting her go, ever. She's just the best thing ever and they're perfect together.'

With thoughts of marriage on his mind, Michael flew back to LA, where work started in earnest for his third album with David Foster.

David's luxury pad in Malibu was becoming a second home to Michael. When the chips were down, when he had been burned by the sting of the press, he was able to return there to find his salvation in music. He hung out in Malibu, discussing the direction of the third album with David (who was a 14-time Grammy winner) and producer/engineer Humberto Gatica. Michael enjoyed a good relationship with his production team: 'We definitely have a great working relationship where I think I interfere just enough! I mean, David is the greatest producer in the world. They're both so amazing, I couldn't do it without them.'

There was one emotion that Michael felt when facing the recording of his third album: fear. He was completely terrified. 'I knew that it had to be better than the first two – that it had to show growth without alienating anyone, and that's a tough line,' he explained. 'So I sat there from the very beginning and came up with the songs, put together the skeleton, and thought about what arrangers I would hire. I even ended up at the mastering session, which artists rarely attend. I wanted to be involved in every aspect because I wanted it to be conceptually beautiful.'

But in many ways, this was a stronger, more confident Michael who approached his third album. As well as his formative years finding his voice and honing his craft as a singer, Michael also had the experience of his first two albums and their accompanying tours. He had made mistakes along the way, but, importantly, he had learned from them. 'I didn't come in with the same kind of desperation that I may have had on the first or second record,' he said to *AP*. 'I didn't come in thinking, "Oh God, please. I hope this does well because I have nothing else and I worked so hard at this." I have come to the point now where I am really allowing myself to enjoy it, really enjoy it.'

Michael had one piece of original material he wanted to include – 'Lost' – but there was also another original song to go on the album. The song was 'Everything', which was inspired by his relationship with Emily. 'I wrote that song about the great happiness of real love, but at the same time I was making a statement about the world,' Michael said. 'We're living in really crazy times, and I wanted to say that no matter what's happening, this person in my life is what really makes it worthwhile.'

But as far as original material went, Michael drew the line at two songs of his own. 'I wouldn't be happy singing all originals. It's just not me,' he said to the *Herald Sun*. 'Maybe that'll bite me in the butt, but my passion is interpreting the greatest songs ever written. I get everyone coming to my show – gay, straight, black, white – and they all bop to the same songs. It's a testament to the music.'

'The record business is in trouble,' he went on. 'One reason is too many artists put out records on which there are one or two great singles, the rest are fillers.

No wonder people went "I don't want to spend $20 for two songs." No wonder they went to the internet and bought songs for 99 cents! It really was important for me to really passionately believe there were thirteen really good songs. Not a skipper. There's much more to lose now. I'm so excited and so terrified at the same time. I don't want people to hate it. I want them to love it. Every artist's nightmare is to be in the "whatever happened to..." file.'

And so, the album had to have a tracklist every bit as delicious as his first two releases. After months of work, Michael's fans would get a taste of that dream.

Track One was 'The Best Is Yet To Come', written for Tony Bennett, who performed it on his 1962 album *I Left My Heart In San Francisco*. But it was another of Michael's idols, Frank Sinatra, who made the song famous and who is, to this day, most associated with it. Frank sang the song under the guidance of Quincy Jones, on his 1964 album *It Might As Well Be Swing*. It was the

last song Frank ever performed live, and the words 'The Best Is Yet To Come' are even inscribed on Frank's tombstone in Palm Springs. Michael's big-band version got his third album off to a swinging start, and the song soon became one of his favourites to sing live.

Track Two was written by Henry Mancini for the 1964 film *The Pink Panther*. Originally called '*Meglio Stasera*', the track was then given English lyrics and re-titled 'It Had Better Be Tonight' and became famous as the music that sometimes introduced *The Pink Panther Theme*. Michael's stomping, big-band version gave the song a big sound.

Track Three was a song that David Foster suggested for the album: 'Me And Mrs Jones', originally sung by Billy Paul. Michael was less than impressed with the choice of track, and wanted to reject it. 'I was like, "This is so cheesy, David!"' Michael said later. But it turned out to be one of his favourites on the record, and gave Michael the chance to show off his silky-smooth Rat Pack-era voice that made so many of his fans weak at the knees.

Emily – who had a great singing voice – was persuaded to sing backing vocals on the track. She wasn't keen to do it, but Michael was insistent that she get involved. 'I heard her sing and went "My God, what do you *not* do?" She even plays the cello, which makes me feel even more insignificant. She did it in one take. She was cringing but it was so good,' Michael said afterwards.

The Leonard Cohen 1988 classic 'I'm Your Man' was chosen as Track Four. Of all the songs on the album, this stood out for Michael as his 'mature moment', helped along by a bluesy arrangement by David Foster. 'I always thought it was a wonderful song – desperate, sexy, and dark,' Michael explained. 'I actually called Leonard and told him I was afraid of performing it live. When he asked me why, I said because he'd written too sexy a song and I was afraid men were going to throw their underpants at me. He just laughed and said, "I wouldn't worry too much about that!"'

Track Five, Mel Tormé's 'Comin' Home Baby' featured Boyz II Men (one of America's original boy bands) sharing lead vocals. Michael found great joy in bringing together a song that was a 1960s hit, a boy band who were massive in the 1980s, and a kid who found fame in the mid 2000s. The song itself was a great and upbeat salsa rhythm, but Michael received criticism for his choice of vocal guests. 'All I know is that they're great singers,' he said, defensively. 'They're artists. They know what they're doing, know what they want. And I just don't give a shit who's hot or who's not.'

Track Six on the album was the ballad he had written as a tribute to his relationship with Debbie, 'Lost'. With its intimate lyrics ('Life can show no mercy, it can tear your soul apart … one thing that's still the same, in my heart you still remain'), 'Lost' was the album's main tearjerker.

'Call Me Irresponsible', the title track and Track Seven of the album, was another made famous by Frank Sinatra, though there had been a number of other versions of the song, which had been originally written in 1962. Michael decided to name the album after this song because it came to represent his opinion on the state of love: either you are in love, he explained, and it's the greatest thing in the world, or you're out of love, and it's the worst thing in the world.

Track Eight on the album was heralded as one of the most ambitious tracks that Michael had ever recorded: a bilingual cover version of Eric Clapton's

# 'I always thought it was a wonderful song – desperate, sexy, and dark'

classic love song, 'Wonderful Tonight', on which Michael duetted with Brazilian jazz legend Ivan Lins. 'How cool is it that here I am, 30 years old from Canada, and I'm singing a song with a 60-year-old man from across the world in Brazil?' Michael exclaimed. 'And he's singing in his language and I'm singing in mine, and we have a perspective that's different because we're from a different generation, and yet we tell a story and it means the exact same thing to both of us. There's a connection there!'

Track Nine on the album was the second original track, co-written by Michael, Amy Foster-Gillies and his musical director Alan Chang and called

'Everything'. It was a song that Michael had started writing aged just 16. Originally the song had been a lullaby, but when Michael sat down with Alan Chang, it was decided to make the song a little more upbeat, and so the inspiration behind the song was Michael's strong relationship with current girlfriend, Emily. 'We changed the feel, and I just wanted it to be a very 1970s kind of summery, really easy-going tune,' Michael told *Deseret News*. 'It's an analogy of what this person is to you, this person in this crazy life that we live – that person who keeps it all together for you.'

Track Ten was 'I've Got The World On A String', a song originally written for the 1932 revue show of Harlem jazz and blues joint, The Cotton Club. There were a number of versions of the song, by famous artists like Louis Armstrong, Ella Fitzgerald and Barry Manilow, but it was Frank Sinatra who recorded the most celebrated one in 1956. Michael sang a jaunty, upbeat version, driven by guest star Joel Peskin on saxophone and background vocals.

Track Eleven on the album was 'Always On My Mind', originally a country song, but one made famous by Elvis Presley in 1972. Michael performed a slow and breathy rendition of the song that was intimate and touching.

Track Twelve on the album was one of Frank Sinatra's most well-known songs, 'That's Life'. Performed on his 1966 album of the same name, the song had been covered by countless artists since then, including Aretha Franklin, The Temptations and Shirley Bassey. Michael's version soon became a live classic. He added a new swinging arrangement that brought the song bang up to date, with a gospel backing choir and some gospel-style rap.

The last track on the original album release was called 'Dream', written by Johnny Mercer in 1944. With some sweeping strings and Michael's gentle vocals, the song brought tears to the eyes of thousands of fans across the world, and was a fitting closure to an emotive third album.

All this after four months in the studio, working tirelessly on the arrangements and shuttling in an impressively huge cast of guest players for the album, among them the Clayton-Hamilton Jazz Orchestra, Brian Bromberg playing bass, Dean Parks playing guitar, Vinnie Colaiuta playing drums, as well as Boyz II Men and Ivan Lins.

As Michael had grown in experience and ability, his opinion now had more weight when it came to key decisions about the album, such as song choices or selecting guest musicians. 'Yes, producers and people at the record company are still trying to control what I do, in some instances very heavily,' he explained to *The Times*. 'I understand they're just trying to do what they think is right and I love that they give me advice – I really do. I'm hungry for their wisdom and knowledge. But it's my face on the CD sleeve and me who wins or loses as a result of what I put out. Having listened, watched and learnt, I now know exactly who I am and what I want to do.'

In the weeks preceding the album's release, Michael wasn't nervous; he was relaxed, because for him, the goalposts had moved. Previously, he had been concentrating on finishing the album, but now he was thinking about the forthcoming tour, and already thinking about his fourth album. His life was about work. 'At no point have I celebrated the success of the past two records and nor will I celebrate the success of this one, if it's successful,' he said.

In the run up to its release, executives at the label were extra cagey about letting anyone have a copy of the album in case it got leaked on the internet. Journalists who wanted to review an advance copy of the album faced a military-style security operation, as the label hosted top-secret, private listening sessions for reviewers, and made sure that none of them were carrying recording devices in their pockets.

It was, Michael thought, a bit ridiculous. 'If I was one of you guys, there would be a part of me going, "What are they hiding?"'

But as the debacle at the Grammys had shown earlier that year, Michael was hot property. At this point, he had sold 11 million copies of his first two albums worldwide. His third album was a very big deal. He was charismatic and charming, as at home on the stage as he was anywhere, and his sense of humour and quick wit had led to his being called one of the world's truly great entertainers. His highly personal interpretations of classic songs gave older audiences something new, while introducing younger audiences to a whole new genre of music. The people who had previously written him off as a karaoke wedding singer were now sitting up and taking notice.

As his popularity skyrocketed, Michael had to learn to deal with the dark side of fame. He was fortunate enough to be guided by celebrities who had had successful music careers in the public eye their whole lives. His friend and idol Tony Bennett advised him 'Don't respond, ever, to anything.'

Michael also learned a valuable lesson from Paris Hilton in dealing with the pressures of fame and the increasing demands of fans. Michael and Paris were both staying at the same hotel in Tokyo, and Michael was impressed at the debutante's impeccable behaviour. 'Even when people were totally out of line, grabbing at and mauling and being rude to her, she never showed attitude or was ever less than gracious. I was so impressed and am trying to learn from that,' he told the *Sunday Times*.

With this humble attitude – and forever trying to watch his mouth in interviews – Michael's hard work on his third album was rewarded. By June, just a couple of weeks after its initial release, *Call Me Irresponsible* had hit the number-1 spot in America, Canada, Australia and across parts of Europe. And as the weeks went by, the album sales kept on racking up. Fourteen weeks after it was released, the album had sold 820,000 copies in America and 1.4 million more worldwide.

It was an incredible feat for Michael, who – after months of preparation – was finally back on the road for the *Call Me Irresponsible* tour. The tour would see Michael and his band travelling across North America through the summer, and then across Europe from October to December, and then back to Canada and the US for the winter months.

Although it was hard work, Michael loved being on the road. He gathered energy from the screaming, sell-out crowds as the tour gained momentum. Off stage and between shows, he was hyperactive and brought his characteristic sense of fun to everything.

In between movie shoots, Emily was able to join Michael for part of the tour, although her attendance wasn't always met with joy from Michael's armies of female admirers, who expressed their love for the singer in numerous ways: by throwing underwear on the stage (always clean, according to Michael), slipping love-notes to his bodyguard to pass on to him, and even giving him stuffed toy animals with recording devices inside that held recorded love messages for the singer.

'They all hate me!' Emily told journalist Jonathon Gatehouse, who interviewed Michael and reviewed a show for *Macleans* in August 2007. As Michael spotted the journalist talking to Emily backstage at his show, his dry sense of humour and sharp tongue once again got the better of him. 'You're not writing about her?' Michael said, in a loud voice. 'No, no, I'm serious. Because it's hard to get laid if people know that I have a girlfriend.' Emily smirked knowingly, while some people who were hanging around backstage looked distinctly uncomfortable.

But Emily was used to Michael's jack-the-lad attitude and dry sense of humour that was often too close for comfort. And despite Michael's odd, misinterpreted joke, the couple were closer than ever. 'He is very content and in love,' confirmed his sister Crystal. 'Every time he sees her on screen he falls in love with her all over again!'

However, the good times weren't to last, as the rock-solid relationship between Michael and Emily was shaken by a shocking revelation.

# trouble in love

I n November 2007, while he was on tour in Europe, Michael's world was rocked when *Hollywood Gossip* published an interview with a woman called Tiffany Bromley, who accused Michael of cheating on Emily – with her!

Taking Tony Bennett's advice about not responding to anything, there was no comment from camp Bublé. There was also no comment from camp Blunt, as Emily's manager advised her not to comment on the story, knowing it would soon blow over.

Though he wouldn't be drawn to comment on the story, Michael retained his trademark sense of humour, though it seemed to only add fuel to the fire. *Blender* magazine issued Michael a series of questions that they went on to publish as a Q&A, and many of his responses were met with raised eyebrows.

Michael's publicist knew that he had weathered greater storms than this – he had managed to come through the Grammy scandal at the start of the year relatively unscathed. Michael and Emily still smiled for the cameras when they were seen together.

Desperately trying to smooth over the rough patch, Michael continued on his tour of the UK. He made a special guest appearance on TV talent show *The X Factor*, where he held a surprise masterclass with the four finalists, Leon Jackson, Same Difference, Niki Evans, and Rhydian Roberts. Knowing that Scottish finalist Leon Jackson was a big fan of his, Michael invited him backstage at Wembley to hang out with his family and Emily while he performed. And Leon couldn't have been more shocked when – in the middle of his set – Michael announced that he had a special guest who was going to come on and perform 'Home' in front of 12,000 screaming fans. Despite the surprise, Leon took the challenge in his stride, belting out a fabulous performance that the fans loved.

'I'd never rehearsed it with him, I never had a soundcheck, I just went up and winged it and it was beautiful, man, a dream come true and when I came off I was a wee bit emotional at the end,' said Leon afterwards.

Michael's special appearance on *The X Factor* did more than just wow the contestants. His album *Call Me Irresponsible* shot up in the UK chart from number 21 to number 3, selling over 100,000 copies following the show. And by January 2008, Michael's star was shining brighter than ever. He had sold over 15 million copies of his albums worldwide. His live tour dates were selling out in a matter of hours, and as soon as more dates were put on sale to satisfy the growing need, they sold out, too!

Michael had over 50 live dates scheduled between January and May 2008, and his schedule was made even more hectic by the addition of numerous awards ceremonies that the roguish singer was invited to.

Michael's cabinets were groaning with all the accolades he was getting for *Call Me Irresponsible*. After the scandal with the 2007 Grammys, Michael kept his mouth firmly shut about his two nominations for the 2008 Awards: Best Male Pop Vocal Performance for 'Everything' and Best Traditional Pop Vocal Album for *Call Me Irresponsible*. He was awarded with a Grammy for the latter.

'Winning a Grammy was a dream come true. It was a first for me and you always remember your first time,' said Michael with a wry grin. 'It makes it doubly exciting to get back on the road to perform for my fans.'

Not satisfied with his first Grammy, Michael also chalked up five nominations in the 2008 Juno Awards for Fan Choice, Single of the Year, Album of the Year, Artist of the Year and Pop Album of the Year. Though he only came away with the Fan Choice award, he also snagged two trophies at the fourth annual Canadian Smooth Jazz awards, winning Male Vocalist of the Year and Best Original Composition for 'Everything'.

The awards ceremonies were calling from overseas, too, as Michael was nominated for Best International Male at the Brit Awards. He eventually lost out to Kanye West, but the show again sent album sales of *Call Me Irresponsible* soaring, and the album jumped back up the UK charts from 14 to number 4.

Though it was wonderful to be recognised by winning awards, Michael's mind was set very firmly on his tour, which took him across North America, playing arena after arena. Unlike many entertainers, Michael had found it easy to adapt to audiences of 10,000 people – it was like he was always born ready for it. 'You just have to be confident enough in yourself as an entertainer to play to every single person in that room, whether it's two hundred people or whether it's twelve thousand,' he said. 'There are entertainers that find it probably easy to play to the back seats ... There's a presence there. I'm not

saying I have it. I'm saying I hope to have it. I don't feel like I had to change much of what I did. I always felt what I was doing in nightclubs was built for an arena, if that makes any sense!'

Michael's *Call Me Irresponsible* tour had been designed to take musical entertainment to a new level of interaction with the audience, as well as giving them all the musical hits they craved. He wandered out into the crowd in his usual way, hugging kids here and there, posing for pictures with fans and kissing screaming women on the cheeks. Michael even had a dramatic interlude planned with his horn section, during which he introduced them, then left the stage amidst a fake tantrum, leaving one of the trombonists in his band, Nick Vayenas, to squeal on him. Nick told the audience that off stage he and the rest of the band weren't allowed to speak to Michael or make eye contact with him. Nick also said that Michael was a giant diva, who lip-synced his way through his shows, and then proceeded to mock-sing 'Fever'. All this to the applause and delight of the audience. Michael then ran back on stage and clipped Nick round the ear, and the two swapped their microphone and trombone and carried on hamming it up for the audience.

The warm reviews for Michael's shows continued as he took the *Call Me Irresponsible* tour to Australia, where legions of Australian Bublé fans were waiting impatiently to see their man. Michael had sold out nearly all of his 17 dates across Australia throughout May and June.

Part of the run on tickets was to do with the ticket price. Due to his increased popularity, Michael had moved from playing stadiums in Australia to playing arenas. On hearing that all the ticket prices in Australia would be $99, Michael spoke with his Australian promoter and requested that the ticket prices be reduced to a more modest $65.

Though most of Michael's entourage – including his father – were against the lower price, Michael stood firm. He had made more money than he ever thought he would, and he had sold more albums than he'd ever dreamed he would, and it was all because his fans had supported him. Many acts that reached the same level of popularity increased ticket prices to make the most of their time in the sun, but Michael had his feet too firmly on the ground to allow himself to do that.

'You can't charge $99 if they're in an arena seventy metres away from you,' he said to the *Herald Sun*. 'I want people to know I'm not ripping them off. Some bands charge $500 a ticket. Who can come to that show? I don't care if Sinatra comes back from the dead, I ain't paying $500 a ticket. It's nice to build an audience slowly. I still feel like the underdog. Even though maybe I'm not, but I still feel like the underdog.'

When Michael made the decision about the ticket prices, he had thought about his own family, with his own father working hard his whole life and making a modest living. He wanted to ensure that people like his own family weren't excluded from his concerts just for the sake of a few bucks.

'It's about showing appreciation to an audience,' Michael went on. 'It's about letting the guy making thirty grand a year come with his family. It's not going to kill him to bring his family. He bought my record, too, so why should he pay $150 for a ticket? I'm not so out of touch with reality to not know it's a big deal to come out to a show. If a family comes there's parking, restaurant, babysitters – that all adds up to a lot of money.'

And Michael, determined to give his fans their money's worth, made sure that he took photos with every fan who wanted one, shook hands with every fan who held theirs out – even allowed his behind to be grabbed and pinched by roving female hands from every audience. At a show in Melbourne, he stopped to chat to a ten-year-old girl, and said that having kids at his show gave him a sense of responsibility that stopped him turning into Amy Winehouse.

'That's the show – I'm cheeky, I'm irreverent, I'm having fun,' Michael said. 'I know there are points in the show when I'm so dorky it's unbelievable. And see, I met the ten-year-old girl and four seconds later a woman grabbed my ass, so it's all kinda strange. In a weird and probably egotistical way I feel that little kid will never forget that. My dad took me to the Harlem Globetrotters when I was a kid and they picked me to throw this bucket of water over. It's still a big deal to me.'

But while Michael was committed to giving his audience the best possible time in his shows, the cracks were starting to appear in his relationship with Emily.

And in July, as Michael embarked on a mini tour of the UK, playing Newcastle, Glasgow, Liverpool, Cardiff and London, news of his official split with Emily hit the gossip sites. This time, the rumour was true. Michael's publicist Liz Rosenberg released a statement to *E! Online* that the couple had split up after being together for three years. 'Sadly, after three years, they have parted ways,' stated Perez Hilton's website. 'They are both extraordinary people with huge talent. Let's wish them well.'

In some ways, the break-up wasn't a surprise. Michael had mentioned in interviews that the couple found it hard to find time to spend together with his intense touring schedule and her shining movie career.

Both Michael and Emily regretted being so open with the media about their relationship because, now that it was over, the break-up heartache was doubly

tough to go through. Emily withdrew completely – both from media interest and from her friends. She kept quiet about their break-up for weeks as it was too painful to tell her friends she was single again. 'A break-up is agonising and it's a horribly anguished thing to go through,' she said. 'It's really tough. From my point of view – why would you make that public? Why would you put it out there for everyone's discussion? It's embarrassing.'

Michael struggled through the rest of his tour, nursing a deeply wounded heart. For months afterwards, in his time off stage, he was suffering from depression. 'I'll go home and I'll curl up in a ball and I'll cry. I'm not kidding. I'll just cry,' he said. 'Emily was a substantial person and amazing still. Top girl. Top class.'

Although Michael refused to comment on exactly why they split up, their careers definitely didn't help things. 'In my business it's tough to go out with another artist because you're never together. You're lucky if you can see the person once every two to three months, and with Em, she was on her movies and I was doing my thing so it made it more difficult.'

Struggling to cope with his workload and his broken heart, Michael turned to therapy to help him, as he thought it was his approach to life that was

harming him. 'I was going through the break-up and asking myself why,' he said to the *Daily Express*. 'I have a tendency to sabotage relationships; I have a tendency to sabotage everything. Fear of success, fear of failure, fear of being afraid. Useless, good-for-nothing thoughts.'

And although the therapy, and the break-up, was painful, it would be one of the most important things that ever happened to him.

# new beginnings

8

ollowing his very public break-up with Emily, Michael was heartbroken. But slowly, and piece by piece, he started putting his life back together. 'When it happened, obviously it was devastating, man,' Michael said later. He had more money and success than he'd ever dreamed of having, but the old saying was true, he learned: money can't buy you happiness.

But the break-up had given him perspective on his life. He had learned that perhaps what he needed in a partner was different from the two women he had occupied his time with before. 'I don't want a pushover. I want a strong human being that doesn't put up with my BS. It turns me on actually,' he said.

But Michael was deeply unhappy. It was all he could do to hold it together for the last of the UK tour dates in July. As the *Call Me Irresponsible* tour reached a hiatus for the summer, Michael returned home to Vancouver, licking his wounds, and spent some time in the loving bosom of his family, and with the open ear of a therapist.

Neither Michael nor Emily would confirm the real reason for the split, both insisting that it was personal and not public business. And though Emily remained silent about the break-up and refused to discuss it, or her own mental state, with the press, Michael – who frequently wore his heart on his sleeve – found it difficult to stay quiet when asked about things. Indeed, he thought that his openness was part of the problem in the first place.

'We were naive, I think. We were both excited about the relationship, and we talked openly about it, and I think we both learned that when you give away even little things, they're not yours anymore. So I've learned just to keep my private life private,' he said to the *Providence Journal*.

Keeping his private life private was advice he had been given by several different people at times in his career, but like most things in life, Michael had to learn the lesson himself before he could truly understand the value of it. And there were other lessons Michael learned from the break-up – and opportunities he took from it.

'It gave me an opportunity to take a good look at myself and to want to change, and to want to become a better guy,' he said to the *Telegraph*. 'I allowed my "fault self" to fill me up. I allowed my insecurity to run my life a little more. And there were a lot of things I did and a lot of mistakes I made that I

## 'I don't think I'll ever lose my edge and my fascination with relationships. The more that I learn, the less I know'

can't take back. So I realise that. And I took the opportunity to learn from it and to grow. I'm a much happier guy. I'm far more content in my life. And the truth is, I like myself. I like myself enough to really like somebody else.'

Michael spent the summer months taking long walks around Vancouver and passing time with his parents in Burnaby. It was time out that he sorely needed from his hectic touring schedule, but by the time October rolled around, he was ready for more concerts.

There was no getting away from the 'Emily' question, though, as journalists probed in interviews, trying to get the real dirt on the split and whether there might be a reconciliation. But any chance of that was scuppered when Emily was spotted out with American actor John Krasinski, famous for his role in the

American version of the *The Office*. Though Michael was enjoying the single life and dating, he wished only the best for Emily in her new relationship. 'I will always love her. We're still friends,' he told *People*, adding: 'I love that guy in *The Office*. He's great.'

'I felt bad for everybody involved,' he said later to the *Age* about the break-up. 'It's definitely worse 'cause it's all done publicly. You go to the grocery store and it's in every magazine. It's the same thing that's happened in my other break-ups. It's always tough. You grow attached to someone and they become your best friend. You lose a friend – that's one of the most difficult parts. I'm a sentimental person. But at the same time it also inspires me to write. It's no different than the regrowth of a forest. Something has to die to regain life again.'

Michael looked to one his childhood loves – ice hockey – to go some way towards healing his broken heart. He invested in the Western Hockey League's Vancouver Giants, in which he became a minority owner.

'I couldn't be more thrilled to be a part of such a wonderful team, management and ownership – a group of winners,' he said. 'I've done lots of amazing things in my life, but this is easily the most prestigious for me. It's a dream come true to be a part of this club. Hockey is a huge part of my life, and I'm sentimental about it, actually.'

'My plans are honestly to watch these boys. As long as they don't tell me what songs to put on my record, I promise I ain't gonna tell them who to put on the ice!' he laughed.

With his hockey fix achieved, Michael felt revived, and reinvigorated to be back on the road as his tour headed to South America. In late November, his record company threw a party for him after a concert in Buenos Aires, Argentina. The head of the label wanted to introduce Michael to Argentina's most famous actress, Luisana Lopilato. Michael was very taken with the gorgeous blonde, and although Luisana's English wasn't great, the pair chatted all night.

Unfortunately for Michael, at the time Luisana was dating tennis player Juan Monaco. So he tried to put thoughts of the actress out of his mind as he continued on his tour. Luisana's publicity rep issued a statement to the gossip rags, stating categorically that there was nothing going on between her and Michael, and that she remained faithful to her tennis-playing boyfriend.

But the pair stayed in contact – and Luisana started taking English lessons, sparking rumours that her romance with Juan Monaco was on the rocks. It was April when, shrouded in mystery, Michael boarded a flight to Buenos Aires for a week. Luisana had split with Juan Monaco, and she invited Michael for dinner at her sister's house. In their initial conversation backstage at his concert, Michael had expressed his desire to taste the meat in the country (as Argentina is famed for its meat). So Luisana arranged a tasty barbecue, complete with a translator to help them communicate. Despite the language barrier, there was strong chemistry between the couple. And if food was the way to a man's heart, then Michael was eating his way into love again.

Very aware of keeping the relationship a secret – and keeping it special – for as long as possible, Michael and the petite blonde denied all rumours of anything going on between them, though the gossip rags in Buenos Aires were full of stories of the actress being spotted out with the singer. And soon, the rumours were impossible to hide, as the couple were snapped in public in Las Vegas in May. Onlookers commented on how cute the couple looked, and noted how Michael couldn't keep his hands off his new girl – a petite blonde bombshell.

But it wasn't just a new love that was keeping Michael busy. He had given himself some time off from his live tour, to concentrate on pulling himself back together after his difficult break-up with Emily, and also to work on his fourth studio album.

Michael had done a lot of growing up over the past year. He had matured and had learned so much about himself – as a performer, as a lover and as a person.

The result was that his thoughts about what he wanted for his next album had changed. He didn't want the perfect, polished finish of his first three albums. He wanted something raw – something that truly tapped into the energy of a live performance.

'Don't get me wrong,' he said to *Sun Media*. 'I'm really proud of my first three records. But they were done in a very slick way. They sound really good; sonically, they're beautiful. They're all about perfection – if something isn't perfect, you pull it out and fix it. There are no mistakes. And as much as I liked them there was something missing for me.'

To try and find what it was that was missing, Michael spent hours and hours poring over some old favourites, albums that he had loved when he was younger, trying to pinpoint what it was about them that he loved so much, and wondering how he could recreate that magic for himself.

He pulled out records by the Beatles, Frank Sinatra and Elvis. He also listened to old Motown compilations, and tried to work out what it was that made the records so legendary, what it was about the music that moved him so much. 'I realised that we live in a Pro Tools, American Idol generation,' he said. 'We've become used to listening to this absolutely perfect music, but the heart and the soul are gone. It's so antiseptic.'

In an attempt to recapture that magical effect that comes from a live performance – and that was so present in the old records that Michael loved so much – he realised that he was going to have to take a completely different approach to recording this, his fourth album.

Some people thought he was crazy. Michael had sold 21 million copies of his first three albums – why mess with the formula? But Michael was adamant. He wanted to do this his way.

He approached David Foster again and told him he wanted to record the album in a different way. He wanted each song recorded live – each instrument in the band to be playing and him to be singing – in just one take. David was uncomfortable at the thought of this. But eventually, after much persuasion, he agreed to give Michael more control over how the new album, tentatively named *Crazy Love,* was going to be produced.

'I think that he put his balls on the line in belief of me and my ideas and my ideology of how I wanted to record this record,' Michael said to the *Vancouver Sun.* 'Because that's just not his style. And he basically gave me the shot. He said, "Okay, man, you want to try this, fine. But, I'm telling you, it's not going to sound the same. You're not going to be pitch perfect."'

But Michael didn't want to be pitch perfect. And so, as a compromise, they decided to split their work on *Crazy Love.* David produced half of the album, but on the other half Michael was free to collaborate with his own musical heroes, inviting Sharon Jones and the Dap-Kings and Naturally 7 into the studio, and covering cult artists like Ron Sexsmith and the Eagles, despite David and manager Bruce voicing their concerns about those choices.

Michael wanted the recording process to be more organic. 'I want to shove those microphones in the room and I want the band just to go in there and play. I don't care if the tempo speeds up or slows down. I just want it to feel great. I want those drums to be bleeding into the bass, and the bass bleeding into the strings, and them bleeding into my vocals. I want this to have some real edge,' he told David, who agreed to let Michael go with his gut.

Michael and David took their new project into the large Warehouse studio in Vancouver. They were accompanied by Michael's band, his engineer Humberto Gatica and producer Bob Rock, and they worked tirelessly on songs that Michael had been putting together since his break-up with Emily. The location was perfect for Michael, as his mother and grandmother could easily get to the studio, and they often came over while Michael was at work and cooked for him and the crew.

Track One on the album – a slow, sultry number about love gone wrong, called 'Cry Me A River' – was made famous by Julie London, who sang it in the 1956 musical romp *The Girl Can't Help It*. Cover versions had been performed by acts from Aerosmith to Etta James, but Michael made the song all his own with the big-band sound he was famed for. 'I wanted it to be really cinematic, really over the top and bombastic – almost like a Bond theme,' Michael explained to the *Pittsburgh Post-Gazette*. 'So I wrote that opening part for it and hoped we could incorporate it into the song and take it to a new place.'

The jazz standard 'All Of Me' was chosen as Track Two. Originally written in 1931, it became one of the most-recorded songs of the 1930s. Frank Sinatra sang one of the best-known versions of the song, and Michael's new arrangement paid tribute to this, through its nightclub piano opening that built into a heavy swing.

Track Three on the album was 'Georgia On My Mind'. The song was originally written in 1930, but hit the charts when Ray Charles recorded a blues version in 1960. Willie Nelson was a particular fan of this rendition of the song, and in 1978 released a country cover. Michael remained faithful to the original flavour of the track, and introduced it to a new generation of fans. 'Whether I write or interpret, I'm trying to be as honest as I can,' Michael said of the song. 'I'm trying to be in the moment and I hope if I believe enough that my audience will believe with me.'

Track Four on the album was by another of Michael's all-time heroes, Van Morrison: 'Crazy Love'. 'When I sing "Crazy Love" it's not that I am going to sing better or sound better than Van Morrison, it's that it's going to be different than Van Morrison,' Michael said about his choice of song. 'It is going to be my interpretation of the song. That can only come from my life experience and what I have gone through. Or the love or the loss I've gone through.'

Track Five was the first of two original songs on the album – a swinging pop song called 'Haven't Met You Yet', which Michael wrote with collaborators Amy Foster-Gillies and Alan Chang. And though Michael had tried to keep his personal life out of his music, it just wasn't always possible, as 'Haven't Met You Yet' had been inspired by new girlfriend Luisana when they had first met, and she featured in the video.

'I wrote it because I had met this girl and there was nothing solid about anything of it,' he stated to the *Age*. 'She didn't speak English. She had just been in a relationship that was very public for her and so had I. There was every reason to not try to get into this predicament of a relationship, yet I did and it was weird. The song came from that – it was inspired by meeting her. You live on your potential as a single person – it keeps you sane,' he says. 'I'm not saying that you can't be alone and be happy but there's this great way to keep your sanity where it's like you know a new relationship is going to happen – you just haven't met them yet.'

Track Six on the album was 'All I Do Is Dream Of You', a song that became popular when Debbie Reynolds sang it in the musical *Singin' In The Rain*. Michael's version remade the song in a 1950s style, which soon became a live favourite.

The second original song was 'Hold On', the album's Track Seven, which Michael wrote again with co-writers Alan and Amy. The song told the story of a couple who break up, but then manage to nurture a lasting friendship.

Track Eight on the album was a song that Michael had to fight to include. It was a cover of the Eagles' classic, 'Heartache Tonight'. Neither Michael's manager Bruce nor his producer Bob Rock liked Michael's version of the song, but Michael knew by this stage that he should trust his musical instincts. 'My manager just keeps saying, "I don't know, I don't know," Michael explained. 'He and Bob said the same thing: "That's the Eagles, man. I just can't get my head around it." But a lot of my friends that are a lot younger, it's their favourite song on the record.'

For Track Nine on the album, Michael took a song made famous by Dean Martin in the 1960s and made it all his own. 'You're Nobody Till Somebody Loves You' was originally written in the 1950s, and had been covered by hundreds of artists, from Sammy Davis Jr to Andy Williams, and from Frank Sinatra to Nat King Cole.

Track Ten on the album featured special guests Sharon Jones and the Dap-Kings, who had worked extensively with Mark Ronson. Soul queen Sharon

coaxed a delicate performance from Michael on the 1960s swing hit, 'Baby (You Got What It Takes)'. The Dap-Kings (who doubled as Amy Winehouse's backing band) added considerable swing to the song, which was one of Michael's favourites on the *Crazy Love* album.

Track Eleven on the album was the 1980s classic 'At This Moment'. The song became famous when it was used in several episodes of the 1980s American sitcom *Family Ties*, featuring Michael J. Fox. Michael had been a fan of the show and the song as a child and so could not pass up the opportunity to give it the Bublé treatment on his fourth album.

For Track Twelve on the album, Michael picked the popular 1920s standard 'Stardust', and invited the vocal group Naturally 7 to the microphones with him. Naturally 7 were a beatbox group who made the sounds of an orchestra using their mouths. But the song almost didn't make it to the album, as David Foster didn't like it. 'I remember taking "Stardust" to Foster and I said, "What do you think?" And he said, "Dude, it's pitchy." And it

# 'If this feels so good to me, if it feels this soulful, other people have got to feel what I'm feeling'

makes you second-guess yourself. But I kept listening to the record and saying to myself, "I'm not crazy. If this feels so good to me, if it feels this soulful, other people have got to feel what I'm feeling. I'm not alone,"' said Michael.

So, he decided to record it anyway. 'I got my eighteen-piece big band, threw them in a room, chucked in the microphones, set up a little vocal booth, and we did "Stardust" with Naturally 7,' he recalled later. 'My rhythm section was ten feet away, and nobody wore headphones, and we played. We played the song three times and we ended up using the first take. It was so satisfying.'

'It's the space between the notes that makes music,' Michael said. 'When I listen to these old records – Sinatra, the Beatles, Elvis, the Motown records – there's this odd presence, the way they recorded it, the way they even recorded the air in the room, you feel like you're there, as opposed to today, where they stick everyone into a separate room, they record it so clean, there's no air, they put everything onto an MP3 file, compress the shit out of it and it sounds perfect ... but it really kills the soul.'

Track Thirteen on the album was a bonus track that Michael had fought to include – a track called 'Whatever It Takes', by the cult Canadian singer-songwriter Ron Sexsmith. Michael also invited Ron into the studio to collaborate on the new version. 'One of the great challenges of a song stylist is to take highly familiar songs and ask myself, can I bring something special to this song?' Michael explained about his decision to invite Ron into the studio to add something extra to the track. 'Otherwise why waste everyone's time in the studio – just go get drunk and sing at a karaoke bar – and I've done that too!'

And while Michael's label might have been nervous about his new and different approach to his fourth album, they needn't have worried. The album outshone all his previous releases, and would ensure Michael was crowned as the king of swing.

# crazy love

9

'**H**aven't Met You Yet', the lead single from *Crazy Love,* was released in August 2009, and was met warmly by critics and fans, who loved its bright and breezy, radio-friendly pop sensibility. The video for the song features Michael shopping for meals-for-one in a super-market (actually the Killarney Market in Vancouver) and daydreaming about meeting a beautiful woman there, played by his partner Luisana. Michael, Luisana and all the staff and customers then begin dancing around the store, and finally move outside to dance in the parking lot where they are showered with confetti.

'Haven't Met You Yet' reached the Top 10 in Australia, Holland, Ireland, Italy, Japan and the UK, and hit the number-1 spot in Canada and America. It got people excited about *Crazy Love*, set to come out in October. The album release would coincide with an appearance on *Oprah* (which cemented Michael in the hearts of housewives, teenage girls and gay men across the US). The album *Crazy Love* sold over 100,000 copies within three days of being released, and smashed into the charts hitting number 1 in Canada, Australia, Italy and Ireland and number 2 in Holland and the UK. Two weeks after being released, the album had sold over 300,000 copies – quite an achievement for an artist who hadn't released anything for over two years.

133

Though Michael was over the moon about the success of his album, there was no time to stop and celebrate. Dates for the 2010 *Crazy Love* world tour were released and sold out within minutes – so Michael added extra dates for the extra demand, which also sold out within minutes.

To promote his new album, Michael spent a little time in the UK towards the end of the year, and got to be a special guest-host on *The Paul O'Grady Show*, where – backed by his full band – he treated the UK to its first live perform-ance of the hit single, 'Haven't Met You Yet'. He also found time to play a live showcase concert for Heart Radio, where a young man called Alfie Palmer introduced himself to Michael as a Michael Bublé tribute act! Michael invited Alfie up on stage to sing 'Home' with him. Ever the joker, and impressed by Alfie's ability, Michael ended up asking him to vacate the stage because he had been too good!

Michael also sang at the Royal Variety Performance and met the Queen (who told him she had his album and enjoyed listening to it), and following his success on *The X Factor* the year before, Michael was invited back onto the show as a celebrity mentor, where he performed 'Feeling Good' as a duet with finalist Stacey Solomon, as well as a steamy solo performance of 'Cry Me A River'.

'There are no guarantees with a show like *The X Factor*,' he advised his mentees. 'Even if you win, it doesn't necessarily mean that you're the most talented singer. It just means you're the best on a particular day. You could win and find your career in tatters four months later. You might also get eliminated, but still end up with a decent career. Chris Daughtry finished fourth in *American Idol* three years ago, but his first album sold a million and he's still doing well now. Leona Lewis has shown she has staying power, too.'

After his whirlwind promotional tour at the end of 2009 – which had taken in America, Canada, Australia and the UK – Michael returned home for Christmas, and spent time over the holiday with his family, and also with his partner Luisana in her home country of Argentina, where Michael had to be accompanied by legions of security guards because Lu was such a big star there. 'You can't imagine,' he told the *Daily Mail*. 'I have to hire security. Like, not just a little bit of security – I have to hire, like, an army. When I'm in Canada, no one follows me. There, the paparazzi will stand in front of the car and then they'll lie on the car so you can't go anywhere. And there are tons of them and they chase you on their bikes … It's amazing. It's like a movie or something!'

In fact, things had been going so well between Michael and Lu that Michael proposed to her in Argentina, in front of her entire family. Everyone burst into tears of joy, they were so happy! Michael then whisked Lu off to Hawaii, where the couple stayed at a Maui beachfront mansion and celebrated New Year's Eve together.

But when asked to give further details about their relationship, Michael was more reserved than he had been when talking about relationships in the past. 'I'll talk as candidly as possible about my feelings but when it gets into personal stuff I think Emily and I learned a heck of a lot when we were together,' he told the *Age*.

'One of the biggest things we learnt was when you speak publicly about your relationship there becomes a greater expectation for you to share more and more. You start to lose these things that are special. All relationships are difficult – I don't care who you are but there are ways to ease the difficulty of it. But I'm always nice about it. I never want to be one of those people who says, "Don't ask me this." This is part of my life. My style is romantic, so I understand.'

Michael gave Lu a diamond engagement ring from Vancouver jeweller Minichiello. The couple immediately began planning their wedding, which soon turned into two weddings: one in Argentina for Lu's close family, and another in Vancouver for Michael's. 'I don't think Luisana really cares where she works, I think she just loves to work,' he said. 'It's the same as me, I don't care what country I'm in as long as I get to do what I love.'

The gossip rags were full of stories of Lu wanting to name their children Bella and Edward after the characters in the *Twilight* saga, and of her demanding a white horse at their wedding ceremony. Michael apparently rejected the idea of the horse, stating that if she was allowed a horse, he wanted to put down an ice rink and skate on it!

But there were some rumours with a bit more truth to them. Michael announced on TV that he would be marrying Lu on 6 April 2011. He then joked that they had planned to get married on 29 April, but decided to change the date after Prince William and Kate Middleton announced the date of their wedding. 'I was going to do it on the 29th, but figured I wouldn't get any press,' he said with a wry smile.

While Michael might have millions of fans across the globe, there was one place he wasn't invited to sing at – and that was his own wedding. He had asked Lu whether she'd like him to sing at their wedding, and she had responded no! 'She said, "I want Ricardo Montaner [a famous Argentine-Venezuelan singer]." So now I've got Ricardo Montaner coming!' said Michael, who was starting to get nervous as the day approached. 'The truth is I know that for a lot of women, this is what they dream of – that day – and I know that that's a big deal for them in their life and they want it to be perfect. I'm a boy, I didn't grow up thinking about my wedding day, so for me, I just want it to be good for her. Really, I just want her to feel like she's had the perfect day,' he added.

## 'I just want her to feel like she's had the perfect day'

The year 2010 was to be an auspicious one for Michael. Not only had he announced his engagement and set a date for his wedding, he also won his second Grammy Award for Best Traditional Pop Vocal Album for a live recording that had been released the year before, titled *Michael Bublé Meets Madison Square Garden*. By February 2010, Michael's releases had sold over 25 million copies since his self-titled debut album was released in 2003.

In 2010, Michael was also nominated for a Brit Award and six Juno Awards, eventually winning four of them (Album of the Year and Pop Album of the Year for *Crazy Love*, Single of the Year for 'Haven't Met You Yet', Artist of the Year and the Juno Fan Choice award). He even got to carry the Olympic torch for part of its journey in Vancouver, and sang at the closing ceremony of the Olympics there.

But the biggest part of 2010 for Michael was his *Crazy Love* tour. Hugely hyped in the media and sold out in seconds, Bublé fanatics around the world screamed and squealed with excitement at the prospect of his return to a venue near them.

At the start of his career, Michael had been partial to the odd dram of whiskey and a cigar to relax after a show. But now Michael preferred to stay sober all the time while touring, to ensure that he was at his best when he was on stage. 'I can't party on tour any more,' he said. 'I think it's part of getting older – you know your limits. I stay sober as I want to put on the best show. It's bigger now, so I need to be sharp.'

And as the tour kicked off, Michael reaffirmed his new, sober status in a phone interview with the *Pittsburgh Post-Gazette*. 'Now I have to be a lot more disciplined. You almost have to be an athlete up there. You can't mess around too much. I want my voice to be strong, and I want my head to be in the right place.'

For the *Crazy Love* tour, Michael's new post-show wind-down routine had changed considerably. To get the adrenaline out of his body, Michael opted to run a few miles on a little treadmill backstage. He would chat with some of the crew, talking to the lighting and sound engineers about what changes they could make to improve the show the following night.

He would also talk to his band and discuss the tempos of the songs, again seeing if there was anything that could be improved for the next show. 'Then I go to my bus, and there's usually a line of a couple hundred people out there, and I sign stuff for them,' Michael added. 'It's a nice way to wind down.' It was a far cry from the nights out that had aided him through his early years in the business.

Though Michael was on tour, he was busy searching for a new home for he and Lu to move into when they were married. But unlike their other pads in Buenos Aires, Vancouver and LA, this new house was in a country that neither of them had any links to: it was a mansion in Surrey! Michael fell in love with the £3-million mansion on the Webb Estate in Purley, and just knew he had to have it.

But he wasn't just spending his earnings on himself. Michael also donated the entire proceeds from a sold-out Vancouver concert to the BC Children's Hospital. He had become an Ambassador for the Campaign for BC Children in 2008, and was passionate about promoting the care of the children at the hospital. 'They are really inspirational people, and the doctors and nurses who care for them are amazing,' he said 'But, when you're in the hospital, you can really understand the need for a new building.'

As the *Crazy Love* tour rolled on, Michael was receiving some of the best reviews of his career. Critics and audiences alike glowed about how he had matured as a performer, and that the young man from Burnaby had transformed from a diamond in the rough to a bonafide superstar.

Michael even broke some personal records when he played to the biggest audience of his career: 45,000 fans at the Aviva Stadium in Ireland. 'I really want to process this, to be connected to all those people, it might never happen again in my life, I can't assume that I'm going to go on to play in a stadium again,' said Michael on the morning of the show. 'I don't ever want to forget these nights.' Although it was a damp day, Michael – ever the gentleman – requested that 13,000 ponchos be distributed to the crowd, to protect them from the wet.

In between the tour dates, Michael also found time to release a new single called 'Hollywood', which was taken from a special, revamped version of *Crazy Love* that was rereleased in October 2010. The new version had an extra CD that featured the new single, an original piece of music written by Michael and Robert Scott.

'My last video and single "Haven't Met You Yet" was about everyone's dream of finding a relationship and love. This time around, it's about celebrity culture and people's dreams about fame and what can go along with that,' Michael said to *PopEater*. 'It's about having fun but remembering where you came from and what's real. You can see how much fun I had playing all those characters.' Among the characters parodied in the video were a pint-sized, floppy-fringed Bublé-Bieber and a rock star in leather trousers, which showed off Michael's thighs to good effect, as well as a Clint Eastwoodesque gun-slinger and a 1970s action hero with a handlebar moustache.

Michael's hard work and the popularity of the *Crazy Love* tour was rewarded in 2011, when the re-released version of the album was nominated for, and won, a Grammy for Best Traditional Pop Vocal Album, and was also nominated for yet another Juno – the Fan Choice award!

Although Michael was on tour at the start of 2011, he was constantly on the phone to Lu and their wedding planners, making sure that everything was

under control for the lavish weddings in April, events that made headlines as weddings of the century.

Although his mind was full of thoughts of weddings and wedded bliss with his betrothed, Michael was also planning and working – not just on his next album, but also planning his future.

'I love the American songbook, and I love interpreting those songs,' he said. 'I would really miss interpreting some great songs. I'm proud to do what I do. I'm proud to be one of the lucky ones who gets to continue the legacy of my idols.'

Though his passion and talent was for interpreting great songs of the past, there were some songs that Michael would never touch. 'There's thousands of songs that are brought to me, and I go, "No! No! Never." Like Sinatra's "My Way" – I can't tell you how many people have come to me with that. I'll never touch that. I'm 34 years old; I'm not ready to sing that song. And even when I am ready, I don't know that I'll touch it,' he explained.

Michael was more confident than ever in his abilities, and his confidence was only growing with every new song he wrote, every album he worked on, and every show he performed.

'I have to believe that you're only as good as your last record, especially in this business now,' he said to the *Pittsburgh Post-Gazette*. 'It's a volatile business and it's harder than ever to sell records. I just don't think you can pat yourself on the back too much. While I appreciate the moment and smell the roses, each time out I put pressure on myself – you gotta be better.'

And so, Michael set himself back to work, determined to produce a new album that was even better than the last. '*Crazy Love* took longer than any of the previous ones and the next one will probably take even longer,' he said. 'It's gotta be right.'

## PICTURE CREDITS

All pictures courtesy of Getty Images

First published in hardback in Great Britain in 2011 by
Orion Books, an imprint of the Orion Publishing Group Ltd
Orion House, 5 Upper St Martin's Lane, London WC2H 9EA

An Hachette UK Company

1 3 5 7 9 10 8 6 4 2

A CIP catalogue record for this book is available from the British Library.

ISBN: 978 14091 4033 7

Designed by carrstudio.co.uk
Printed and bound in Italy

MIX
Paper from
responsible sources
FSC® C015829
FSC www.fsc.org